The series editors:

Adrian Beard is Head of English at Gosforth High School in Newcastle-upon-Tyne, and a chief examiner for A-Level English Literature. He has written and lectured extensively on the subjects of literature and language. His publications include *Texts and Contexts* (Routledge).

Ronald Carter is Professor of Modern English Language in the School of English Studies at the University of Nottingham, the editor of the Routledge INTERFACE series and co-editor of the Routledge Applied Linguistics series. He is author of *Vocabulary* (2nd edn; Routledge, 1998) and co-author of *The Routledge History of Literature in English* (2nd edn; Routledge, 2001). From 1989 to 1992 he was seconded as National Director for the Language in the National Curriculum (LINC) project, directing a £21.4 million in-service teacher education programme.

Angela Goddard is Senior Lecturer in Language at the Centre for Human Communication, Manchester Metropolitan University, and was Chief Moderator for English Language A-Level Project Research for the Northern Examination and Assessment Board (NEAB) from 1983 to 1995. She is now chair of examiners for A-Level English Language. Her publications include *Researching Language* (2nd edn; Heinemann, 2000).

Core textbook:

Working with Texts: A core introduction to language analysis (2nd edn; 2001)
Ronald Carter, Angela Goddard, Danuta Reah, Keith Sanger, Maggie Bowring

Satellite titles:

The Language of Sport
Adrian Beard

The Language of Politics
Adrian Beard

The Language of Advertising: Written texts
Angela Goddard

Language and Gender
Angela Goddard and
Lindsey Meân Patterson

The Language of Magazines
Linda McLoughlin

The Language of Poetry
John McRae

The Language of Conversation
Francesca Pridham

The Language of Newspapers
Danuta Reah

The Language of Humour
Alison Ross

The Language of Drama
Keith Sanger

The Language of Fiction
Keith Sanger

The Language of ICT: Information and Communication Technology
Tim Shortis

Related titles:

English in Speech and Writing
Rebecca Hughes

Alphabet to Email
Naomi S. Baron

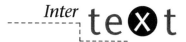

The Language of Speech and Writing

• Sandra Cornbleet and Ronald Carter

Routledge
Taylor & Francis Group

LONDON AND NEW YORK

First published 2001
by Routledge
2 Park Square, Milton Park, Abingdon,
Oxon, OX14 4RN

Simultaneously published in the USA and
Canada
by Routledge
270 Madison Ave, New York, NY 10016

Reprinted 2003, 2005, 2006 (twice), 2007,
2008

*Routledge is an imprint of the Taylor & Francis
Group, an informa business*

© 2001 Sandra Cornbleet and Ronald Carter

Typeset in Stone Sans/Stone Serif by Keystroke,
Jacaranda Lodge, Wolverhampton
Printed and bound in Great Britain by
TJ International Ltd, Padstow, Cornwall

British Library Cataloguing in Publication Data
A catalogue record for this book is available
from the British Library

*Library of Congress Cataloguing in Publication
Data*
A catalogue record for this book has been
requested

ISBN 10: 0–415–23167–1
ISBN 13: 978–0–415–23167–1

contents

acknowledgements

Thanks to all the staff and students in the English Department of Blackpool Sixth Form College. Also to the Leicester group 2000 of Open University students on course U210 and undergraduate students in the Department of English Studies, Nottingham University for their permission to use texts and for their time and help.

The authors and publishers wish to thank the following for permission to reprint copyright material:

Alliance and Leicester for 'House of Happiness'; Daewoo UK; Alfa Romeo UK; Trader Xtra for 'First impressions'; Coldseal Ltd for 'Window problems?'; The Gadget Shop Ltd; Haburi.com; Cambridge University Press.

Every effort has been made to obtain permission to reproduce copyright material. If any proper acknowledgement has not been made, or permission not received, we invite copyright holders to inform us of the oversight.

introduction

This book explores the nature of speech and writing and the overlaps between spoken and written language. We do not normally think much about speech and speaking. When we speak, we do so largely automatically and unconsciously but when we write, we have to be much more aware of what we are doing. Do we type it or write it? Do we send a card or handwrite a letter? Is the message better as an email? Why? And how does the language change? This book aims to make us think more about written and spoken language.

We normally don't learn to write until we are already able to speak. Speech comes before writing. While there are some languages which are only written and which are used mainly for ceremonial or religious purposes, it is almost impossible to imagine a society which only communicates through writing. On the other hand, in the history of civilisation there have been many societies which have relied only on oral communication and many languages today are used without there being a written record. Why? Here we explore the consequences of speech coming before writing. During the course of an average day we also speak much more than we write. This book explores the dominance of spoken language in everyday communication.

Yet most societies value writing more than speech. Most examinations test knowledge by means of reading and writing tasks and most examinations, including the driving test, cannot be passed without competence in the use of written language. The most highly valued texts in most societies are written texts. The term literature is used to refer to written material, including dramatic texts. Why? In this book we examine some of the reasons for the high prestige of writing.

Speaking can often be difficult. We can have false starts, repeat ourselves, forget what we wanted to say, but, generally, speaking is easier to learn than writing. Learning to write requires us to be more conscious of what we are doing and, from the early stages of forming letters to the more advanced stages of moving from one style to another, the process has to be learned and practised before we get proficient. This book investigates the difficulty of writing.

Even though it is difficult to learn to write, the medium of writing is often lacking when you want to express feelings or give emphasis to something. Punctuation such as using capitals or exclamation marks helps but does not help much. Speech very often consists of spontaneous, unplanned face-to-face communication and is a much richer resource for getting your message across. In addition to language, a range of other means is open to us when we communicate face to face. And that includes using silence.

The choices between spoken and written language are normally obvious. For example, if you don't want to risk someone hearing or overhearing what you want to say, then you write a note. If you are a long distance away in time and space and can't access any electronic communication, you have no choice but to write. In *The Language of Speech and Writing* we explore the consequences of the choices between spoken and written texts.

There are, of course, many links between speech and writing. There are many written messages such as text messages on mobile phones, emails or communications on computer chat lines which work like spoken language. And if we want to give a talk to a group of people or to a large audience, the chances are that we'll write down in advance what we plan to say. Most political speeches are written to be spoken and are carefully crafted texts, even if they are written to sound spontaneous. Why? What are the continuities and overlaps between spoken and written language?

The book does not aim to make you write or speak better but it does include a wide range of tasks to help you understand the use of written and spoken language. And a better, more explicit understanding and conscious awareness of language often do lead to a more effective use of language.

When using this book, it is important to be aware of the difference between the following pairs of terms:

Top down and bottom up

It will be obvious from a review of the *Intertext* series alone that linguists love name pairs! Top down and bottom up have nothing to do with standing on your head or turning somersaults – they are, instead, approaches to text analysis. Working from lower level items upwards to the text as a complete unit is looking at texts bottom up; that is, paying attention to the component parts – spelling, grammar, sentence construction, paragraphing, etc. – which build up incrementally to from a written text. Alternatively, we can look at a text as a whole, top down, to consider the genre, style, readership, etc. in order to tease out how it has been created. This would be a top-down approach.

Both of these approaches will need to be kept in mind throughout the investigations in this book of written and spoken texts as they will both be appropriate for different purposes.

Text and discourse

Text can be used for both written and spoken language. It usually refers to a stretch, an extract or complete piece of writing or speech. Texts generally adhere to broad conventions and rules which determine the language and structure used in particular text types. Discourse is a much wider term. It can also be used to refer to language in action, such as legal discourse, which has characteristic patterns of language. Discourse studies look at how writing, and speech, is patterned and linked across the text as a whole.

Sentence and utterance

In spoken discourse analysis, it's more common to refer to an utterance – a stretch of language orally produced – than a sentence, which is a grammatical construct. We do *not* set out to speak in sentences – in fact, in informal speech we rarely do that – rather, we set out to achieve a purpose which may or not require full, accurate sentences: 'speech is characteristically used in pursuit of a purpose . . . The practice of inventing a sentence . . . is a practice of the sentence grammarian, not the user' (Brazil, 1995, pp. 26–7).

Exchange and conversation

Conversation is a social activity between two or more people. It usually involves hopping to and fro in speech over a period of anything from a few minutes to several hours. Within a conversation, a pair of utterances between the parties is known as an exchange.

The nature of writing

This unit aims to investigate:

◎   the nature of writing;
◎   some sub-divisions of writing;
◎   the process of writing;
◎   ways in which writing is taught and learnt;
◎   some of the main features of writing.

What is writing?

Writing is all around us. We *see* written texts every day, even if we don't always *read* them. We write something every day, from a quick shopping list to an academic essay. We all *know* what writing is, somehow, but could we define it precisely?

Activity

Write a one-sentence definition of writing *without* looking in a dictionary. Then compare with other people. What **synonyms** appeared? Can you think of any other synonyms (or near synonyms)?

Commentary

Chambers English Dictionary gives this definition of writing:

> **write** *v.t.* to form (letters or words) with a pen, pencil,
> or other implement on a (usu. paper) surface: to express
> in writing: to compose: to draw, engrave, etc.: to record: . . .
> to indicate (a quality, condition, etc.) clearly: to
> communicate, or to communicate with, by letter. – *v.i.* to perform,
> or to practise, the act of writing: . . . to compose . . .

The range is huge – from letter formation to (creative, original) com-position. So writing isn't easy to define. It's impossible to come up with a simple, one-dimensional answer to the question 'What is writing?'.

Activity

Think back to when you first learnt to write. Try to remember what you were taught and how you felt at the time.

- ◎ *What?* What exactly were you taught? Letter shapes and sizes? Capitalisation? Cursive writing? One handwriting style? Were you continually corrected?
- ◎ *Where?* Were you taught at home or at school or both? Did you feel comfortable in those surroundings? Did your environment affect your ability?
- ◎ *Who?* Who taught you? Did you like the teacher and the teaching methods? Why/why not?
- ◎ *How?* How were you taught? Did you have special handwriting books? Did you copy a model from a book or the board? Were they single letters, words or full phrases or sentences? Could you practise free writing?
- ◎ *Attitude and emotion* How did you feel when you were learning to write – puzzled, frustrated, confident, interested, bored, motivated?

Commentary

We saw in *Chambers Dictionary* that the first definition was 'to form letters or words'. Handwriting is one of the first things we learn to do at school in relation to writing and the physical manipulation, involving motor

6

control and eye–hand co-ordination, must be mastered before going on to anything else. Today, of course, we aren't restricted to writing only by hand in order to produce written texts; texts are produced by printing and electronic methods. The term **graphic** can be used to incorporate all of these. However, these various techniques aren't equivalent to each other. They will produce or avoid certain features of language and text production which we'll consider later. **Graphology**, at any rate, is just one of the many component skills, known as **sub-skills**, of writing.

In your discussion, you may have mentioned some of the sub-skills involved in writing. Some of these are generally taught at an elementary level such as:

◎ spelling;
◎ punctuation;
◎ capitalisation;
◎ grammar.

You may have been taught certain spelling rules, such as '*i* before *e* except after *c*'. At a later stage, this may have been extended to 'and before *ght*'. Later still you will have come across numerous exceptions to the rule! You may have been taught how to use the apostrophe and semi-colon. You'll have been taught when, and when not, to use capital letters. You might have also been taught some grammatical terminology, some **meta-language**, such as the terms 'noun', 'pronoun', 'verb', 'preposition', etc. Many of these are fairly rudimentary but of course throughout your education, and your life, you keep refining, adding to and subtracting from this knowledge as new expressions and new vocabulary are learnt and different skills are needed.

Other writing sub-skills which usually form part of later education processes are organisational features, such as sentence and paragraph construction, link words such as 'although', 'nevertheless' and **cohesive devices** like demonstrative pronouns (*This* theory . . .) etc. Later still, you'll probably have been taught some of the requisites and conventions of text structure and different text types, as, for example, the organisation of information, degrees of formality, style and register, layout and **formulaic expressions** (Dear Sir/Yours faithfully). So we all learn the fundamentals of writing from formal instruction. But we also acquire and refine many skills from our daily experiences.

Writing, as we've said, is therefore *not* one-dimensional. There are many aspects to consider of this very common, quite normal everyday activity.

Activity

The two texts given are notes written by different students for the same teacher. Read them and pick out the various features of the written medium, the different sub-skills, which are represented here. Use the list above as a guide but others should come to light.

Text: Letter 1

Dear Jacqueline,

I can't attend your lesson today as I have an important appointment at the Sports Injury Clinic.

Apologies,

Sarah Granger.

Text: Letter 2

11/5/98

Dear Jackie Shepherd,

I am writing to apologise for not attending your lessons last week. This was due to some confusion on my part as I believed my lectures all started this week. I am very sorry.

Yours Sincerely,

Wood

(SUSAN WOOD)

Commentary

These two letters, left as brief notes in a tutor's pigeonhole, reveal many of the features we've already identified:

◎ Handwriting – Differing styles of letter formation and connection between letters. Some slips and crossings out in the hurry of the writing process.

◎ Spelling – No errors – variations in use of contractions ('can't') as opposed to full forms ('I am writing', 'I am very sorry'). Knowledge of spelling rules in relation to morphological variations e.g. write > writing, confuse > confusion, apology > apologies.

◎ Punctuation – Commas used in both letters after the greeting and closure; full stops at ends of sentences; apostrophe. Capitalisation of names of people and the clinic; conventional use of 'Dear' and of closures, though non-standard use of 'Sincerely'.

◎ Grammar – Full sentences in standard grammar with standard word order.

◎ Verbs – Manipulation of various verb forms: infinitive ('to apologise'), gerund ('for not attending') and tenses: past ('believed', 'started') and present tense for future time ('as I have').

◎ Sentence construction – Complex sentences with dependent clauses ('as I believed', 'as I have').

◎ Use of cohesive devices – 'This was due' – 'This' refers back to 'not attending your lessons' (**anaphoric reference**).

◎ Format – Letter format with greetings and closures and positioning of first sentence beneath surname. Text 2 includes the date and a proper signature, with the name printed in block capitals in parentheses beneath.

◎ Style – Text 2 is more formal than Text 1. The formality is achieved through the phrase grammar, lack of contractions, vocabulary, sentence construction and conventional closing. Text 1 is more direct, more informal, with contractions and the abbreviated note style of the closure.

◎ Structure – Text 2 has a conventional formal letter structure: opens with a statement of the purpose of writing, states what has happened and explains the reason, follows with a repeated apology. Text 1 states a future event, gives the reason and offers an apology.

Two written texts, written to the same person, via the same channel, for broadly similar purposes, displaying many similar features and yet also having many distinctive features which set one apart from another.

Other features of writing

Writing is permanent

We commit writing to paper (or any other technological substitute). The physical, concrete reality remains forever, unless some external force intervenes – natural decay, fire, computer crash!

Writing can survive for centuries, for example, the Rosetta Stone, the Dead Sea Scrolls and, perhaps, the year 2000 millennium time-capsules. Writing lives on as a testament to the thought of an earlier time, not just for historical documents but for the diary we wrote yesterday. It provides concrete proof that we can refer back to again and again.

Writing something of such permanence, for essentially anyone to be able to read, gives it a weighty importance which might affect the language used.

Writing is distant

We often, though not always, write in order to communicate with someone else. It stands to reason that if the person we want to communicate with is in the same room, we probably don't need to write to them (unless to keep something private from another party). Written messages are not only conveyed through time but also through space. We can write to someone next door or on the other side of the world.

The first time we sent an email, we talked of sending it 'out into the ether', uncertain if it would be received at all and what the response would be – we couldn't *see* the reader and the reaction the message provoked. It's just the same with other forms of writing – we compose, we trust that the message conveys what we intended and that the response is the one desired.

Writing is planned

Writing takes time. The word 'discoloration', for example, takes the average person approximately five seconds to write but only one second to say. The physical pace of writing, which even with a keyboard is slow, allows for ongoing thought and planning *during* the writing process. As we write a sentence, we can think of each word before we write it and then we can always go back, correct it or alter it, until we're satisfied. Before we can write anything, even a shopping list, we need to think. We can write very little of any length or sense without giving it *some* thought beforehand. Obviously, more important documents need much greater planning.

Writing is formal

Because of all these previous attributes, writing tends to convey important messages and therefore we probably usually write in quite a formal way. The letters we've seen, even though they were quick notes, are both fairly formal and again, the more important the document, the more formal it will be.

Writing is linear – or is it?

As you're reading this, your eye is moving from left to right. Writing in English can be said to be linear: we start on the left-hand side of the page, and move in a straight line to the right. We write one word, followed by another and then another. English is known as an SVO language: Subject – Verb – Object, this being the most common grammatical ordering. So the subject comes before the predicate, prepositions come before nouns, as the name implies (some languages have post-positions). We sequence information in a forward progression: state the cause and explain the effect (though these could easily be reversed and yet still push the text forward). All this seems to imply a straightforward movement from start to finish, left to right, beginning to end. But is it really such a direct route?

Writing is a process

Look again at the two texts on p. 8, at the slips and crossings out. Put yourself in the writers' shoes: we may write a word, re-read it, correct a slip, go on, stop, re-read to check the sense and decide on the best way to proceed and so on. So in some ways, it's more of a cyclical process.

We're so accustomed as readers to dealing with the final product of writing that we rarely consider the process – for that's what writing is, a process. Only when we struggle to produce a text ourselves or when there's something out of the ordinary in a text – some slip or something out of place which has been left over from the writing process – is our attention drawn to it.

Such re-working, isn't restricted to the realms of a literary genius – it's part of the writing process for everyone. So, although slips can, and do, still get overlooked and carried over into final print editions, crossings and scribbles do not normally appear. We've said that writing is planned – but some is more planned than other! So it's not just the fact that machines have a great ability to remove all traces of undesired elements; it's also the fact that casual notes are produced in real time, that is at the time of creation without much review. This is in contrast to the more planned and reviewed nature of more important printed text. We'll consider this in more detail in Unit 5.

Activity

Think about what you did yesterday (or one day recently). List anything, however trivial, you did which involved writing. Compare with a neighbour and then, if possible, discuss in a whole group. You could conduct a class survey to find the most common types of texts, with their average length, as well as the least common texts.

Three influential factors

In a survey we conducted for students, and in addition to coursework, the most commonly written text was a note for a family member. Many also wrote various lists of items or figures at work. And we shouldn't forget the all-important order for the Chinese takeaway!

One student was absolutely adamant that she'd written nothing at all but on later, closer questioning, she realised she'd done the following:

1   scribbled a quick note to pin on the fridge;
2   filled in a cheque;
3   written a list of figures on an account sheet.

Taking these three as examples, we're going to find again and again that the following are vital considerations:

context   purpose   receiver (reader/listener)

Keep these in mind as you study these texts.

Example 1

Hair 11.30
Book train tkt – Mon 6/Fri 10
Milk, butter, yog.

The note on the fridge door was written to the student herself. We tend to think of writing as a method of communication between writer and reader/s but very often these are one and the same person. We write shopping lists, to do lists, diary appointments, notes from phone calls, etc. The purpose of the fridge note, as with these just mentioned, was to remind, and we can see a similar function in the other examples too – we'll come back to this later, as the memory aid function of writing is central and relates to the permanency of writing, as we've mentioned.

Example 2

Filling in a cheque isn't such a personal, private activity. Rather than a personal or social function, it's done in order to carry out a business transaction and is therefore termed **transactional** in nature. The readership is not as simple as it may seem (and, of course, will vary according to the type of cheque): of a cheque sent to another individual or company, naturally the payee will be the primary reader but no action occurs until the payee presents the cheque to the secondary reader, the bank teller, who will then complete the transaction. Dual, or multiple, readership will later be found to be very relevant for other kinds of texts as well, such as novels.

A cheque has more or less a standard format. The layout and design are fairly universal. Space is restricted; imagination is not required. The amount of writing required on a cheque is strictly limited and constrained by prescribed and long-established conventions and, as a result, the actual *reading* involves no more than a cursory check for accuracy. Thus, context and text type (or **genre**) affect language and will need further investigation too.

Example 3

The list of figures on an account sheet demonstrates several points: first, writing is not just about lexis. All kinds of non-lexical communication can take place with other forms – consider figures, charts, graphs, alpha-numeric combinations (as with document numbers), as well as whole systems which have developed based on pictographs, hieroglyphs, and so on.

Context

Context determines meaning. The sentence 'Shackles to be used for lashing purposes only' sounds rather vicious and brings various images to mind! Given the context – the roof-rack of a Red Cross van – the intended meaning is conveyed. So the physical environment in which the text is created and presented is vital and will affect the nature of the writing. Any given topic, wildlife, for example, can be written about in totally different ways according to the context – that of a dictionary, expert journal, children's story etc. The context also relates to the overall communication event – is a letter, for example, initiating communication or in response to another letter? Is a report concluding a business transaction or is it making preliminary proposals? In our three text examples, we have different contexts for each:

1   personal, kitchen, one-off message;
2   setting unknown (immaterial), cheque book environment, response to external event;
3   office; accounts ledger; standard, restricted practice.

Purpose

All communication is purpose-driven. We have a purpose in mind for communicating in the medium and style we choose. That purpose may or may not be achieved, or received, as we expected, but it still underlies the message. The purposes of the three text examples are:

◎   to act as a reminder;
◎   to conduct a real-world business event;
◎   to provide a permanent record.

Receiver

The receiver of a written text is obviously the reader but it isn't always as easy as it might appear to identify precisely who the reader is. We might, when we write, have one very definite person in mind who does in fact turn out to be the reader but that isn't always the case. Sometimes there's a series of readers, some expected, some not. The reader might not be the one for whom the text was originally intended.

The word 'readership' is more accurate in covering a range from

self → known (specific) reader/s → unknown (general) reader/s

In the case of our examples, the intended readership is as follows:

1   the writer was writing for herself; all of us have now read it;
2   if to settle a bill, the cheque will be read by any number of unidentified company officials before or after bank officials; a personal cheque will be read by the payee first and then the above;
3   company personnel; possibly customers.

We should remember that when texts are used for other purposes, such as for language study, they then have unintended readers who read for quite different purposes – purposes for which the texts were not originally created.

Putting all this together and reducing things slightly, we get Table 1.1.

Table 1.1 Context, Purpose, Receiver

Context	Purpose	Receiver
personal, kitchen	memory aid	self
business	transactional	payee, bank official/s
work, accounts ledger	permanent record	company

Conclusion

It's impossible to find a conclusion which answers once and for all the question 'What is writing?' We need to keep in mind the distinction between the mechanics of writing and the psychological processes involved. We've seen that:

◎   writing is planned;
◎   writing is permanent and crosses the boundaries of space and time;
◎   writing is a process made up of numerous sub-skills;
◎   all communication is purpose-driven and our purpose will determine:

   ◎   whether we communicate in writing or speech;
   ◎   the genre;
   ◎   the format;
   ◎   the style and language;

◎   all communication takes place within a context which will give rise to different text types and different language;

◎   texts are written to be read: they have an intended readership in mind.

To gain more insight into how all of these combine to influence the language of writing, we will need to explore different writing activities and texts in more depth. This we do in Unit 3, after we've taken a look at what happens with speaking.

Extension

Look in newspapers and magazines for advertisements which make unusual use of the written medium. Or look in the Yellow Pages or on shop fronts for the names of businesses which also make unusual use of the written medium. Try to categorise them as to language feature, e.g. punctuation, spelling, ambiguity of meaning, use of typeface or font size, unexpected handwriting. Correct them so that they become what people generally expect from a polished final version. What happens when they are re-written or corrected? What are the reasons for displaying unusual or unexpected forms of written language?

The nature of speaking

Aims of this unit

In Unit 1 we looked at the distinctive features of writing. This unit aims to parallel this by looking at the following:

- ◎ the nature of speaking;
- ◎ some aspects of the speaking process;
- ◎ some of the main features of speech activities;
- ◎ CPR (Context, Purpose, Receiver) in relation to speaking.

What is speaking?

The telecommunications company, Orange, claims that 'the most natural way to communicate is simply to speak'. (Well, they would, wouldn't they?) It's true that most young children acquire the ability to speak quite naturally and most of us could get by in general terms without formally being taught how to speak. Just as the rudiments of writing begin with motor control and co-ordination to produce a graphic system, a speaker first of all has to produce sound by controlling the various aspects of the human anatomy and physiology involved in speech production.

Of course, when we speak, a great deal more than just the mouth is involved: the nose, pharynx, epiglottis, trachea, lungs and more. Such a highly complex and sophisticated mechanism produces, even in the most nonsensical utterance, a vast range of highly-controlled sound and air combinations which result in speech. And speaking isn't *just* about making sounds. Birds, animals, babies make sounds and, though it may be communication of sorts, it's *not* speaking.

Activity

As we did with writing in Unit 1, try your own definition without using a dictionary. What is speaking?

Commentary

Even if you had consulted a dictionary, it might not have been all that helpful. *Chambers English Dictionary* states:

> **speak** *v.i.* to utter words: to talk: to discourse:
> to make a speech . . . – *v.t.* to pronounce; to utter:
> to express: to declare: to mention

It's little more than a list of synonyms, and some debatable at that. Does it really tell us what speaking is? We can 'utter words' – for example, 'fish', 'avenue', 'definite' – but that's not really speaking. We can add grammar – to use world-famous linguist Noam Chomsky's much-quoted example 'colourless green ideas sleep furiously' – but it still isn't speaking.

We can attempt a closer definition by saying that speaking is combining sounds in a recognised and systematic way, according to language-specific principles, to form meaningful utterances.

Simply sounds?

Speech is made up of a combination of features:

◎ Sounds – individual phonemes combine to form words. A phonetic alphabet is used to represent sounds in writing as, particulary in English, sounds and spelling don't always correspond (hymn = hɪm). When we listen to speech, we manage to work out the meaning even if the sounds, in isolation, could be confused. Many standard jokes are founded on phonetic ambiguity:

Knock, knock
Who's there?
Letters
Letters who?
Letters in

being based on the similar pronunciation of 'letters' and 'let us'.

- Intonation – in English, there are two basic patterns: rising and falling. The voice falls to mark the end of a syntactic boundary (phrase or clause) – 'I didn't know' ↘ 'if you'd want to help' ↘ but rises to indicate the speaker's intention to continue, to indicate a question (in some but not all cases) or to reflect attitudes such as surprise and disbelief – 'really?' ↗.

- Rhythm – English is a stress-timed language (compared to French, for example, which is syllable-timed). This means the timing of the language and the rhythm are created according to the position of stress within a single word or a group of words e.g. respon´sible; What´ did you say?

   Stresses within words have fixed positions (although occasionally they shift over a period of time e.g. contro´versy > con´troversy) but stress within a group of words can move according to meaning:

   | What´ did you say? = | either 'I didn't hear' or 'I can't believe you said something so rude' |
   | What did you´ say? = | 'How did you personally respond to the other person?' |

   To maintain the rhythm, English has weak and strong sounds:

   It was a gréat évening.

   'was' and 'a' are pronounced very weakly, with short vowel sounds, as is common with grammar words as opposed to content words which carry the meaning ('great evening').

- Pitch – the voice can get louder or softer for a variety of reasons: mood, emphasis, content, e.g. asides are generally spoken much more quietly than the main theme.

- Pace – this is often related to pitch, e.g. louder speech tends to be slower (content words, emphasis) while softer speech is usually faster (asides, grammar words).

Developing speaking skills

What we want to do with speaking changes as we develop. Young children have limited needs and limited reasons for communicating.

Their language, therefore, revolves very much around themselves and anything which they directly come into contact with. They will use pronouns ('me', 'you') and refer to objects in their immediate environment ('dog', 'train'), often using common diminutives or pet names ('doggie' or 'bow-wow', 'choo-choo'). The language is often related to physical needs, of eating, drinking, going to the toilet. It's so immediate, in fact, that children's language is often referred to as 'the here and now'.

As we get older, of course we have more complex needs and desires – to form relationships, to impart and gain knowledge, etc. – and we have more abilities: to conceptualise something which isn't physically present, to theorise about possibilities rather than keeping to the concrete, to express a range of emotions, and so on. Some of these things we can manage to perform fairly successfully on our own but as we grow up and find ourselves in more and more different situations or with differing needs, two things happen:

1   We may need expert training – we can take lessons in how to speak in public or how to perform well in an interview. We can practise oral presentations at school or role-play talking in awkward situations.
2   We build up our skills experientially. We put our foot in it on one occasion and learn how to be more diplomatic the next. We give our friends verbal instructions on how to get to our house but they get lost! We manage better the next time. We don't persuade our parents to buy us some new clothes one day but we learn some successful strategies the next time (or the time after that).

Appropriateness

All through our lives, we constantly change the way we speak and what we speak about and we develop varying degrees of awareness of how to speak appropriately in different situations and to different people, with varying degrees of formality. These are the fairly sophisticated skills which, when not possessed fully, make us stand out in a crowd as childish or naïve or uneducated.

Appropriateness is a key issue. How many times have parents told us not to speak about a certain subject or use certain words/expressions in front of someone or in a particular setting? Most of us manage to judge with greater and greater ability what is or is not appropriate in a given situation, to learn from our experience and feelings, for how we feel when we're involved in various speaking activities also changes.

Discuss the following questions either in pairs or small groups or make notes on your own. During your early schooldays were you involved in any of these activities? If so, (a) how did you feel the first time and (b) how did you adapt after that?

◎ A teacher asked you a difficult question in front of the rest of the class.
◎ You were asked to role-play a scene in class with school friends.
◎ You had to see the head teacher for a private interview.
◎ You had to give an unwelcome instruction or piece of information to the class.
◎ You had to give an oral presentation, a talk of some kind to:

    ◎ your class;
    ◎ groups of classes or the whole school;
    ◎ a school committee or social group;
    ◎ another school, in front of strangers.

How do feelings in these situations differ from how you feel when you do the following:

◎ chat with your friends going home after school;
◎ get home and tell your family about your day;
◎ phone a distant relative to thank them for a gift;
◎ tell a story (of what happened the night before) in front of a large group of friends;
◎ read a story to a little child?

Would you ever/never do the following:

◎ phone a TV programme to enter a phoneline competition which would be broadcast;
◎ phone a radio station to enter a competition or tell a funny anecdote;
◎ appear live on TV in a game show;
◎ go on a TV chat show, such as *Ricki Lake*, to tell your personal problems?

Explain your reasons.

Commentary

In your discussion, some of the following issues may well have come to light:

◎ most people tend to feel more at ease talking with, or in front of, people we know well rather than strangers;
◎ we tend to prefer small groups rather than large;
◎ we usually prefer to keep personal matters amongst our intimates;
◎ we can normally function better with informal rather than formal situations;
◎ we would usually try and avoid confrontational or awkward situations.

And, especially when we're younger, we tend to think we're alone in feeling like this and that everyone else is more confident and skilful.

Context, purpose, receiver

In Unit 1, we considered the importance of CPR (Context, Purpose, Receiver) in relation to written texts, so now we can do the same for speaking.

Context

All language is created in context and the context gives language meaning. Language and grammar books are full of sentences taken out of context which seem meaningless but, once set in context, they are perfectly intelligible. The isolated phrase 'it's parked' would seem to be related to cars but it sounds odd in the passive voice, present simple tense.

> CALLER: Can you check a number for me? I just keep getting an engaged tone.
> OPERATOR: [later, after checking] Yes, it's parked.

In the original telephone context, the meaning, obvious to telephone operators and part of their jargon (at least at the time, which was a few years ago), becomes clearer i.e. the receiver hadn't been replaced properly.

Context relates to both the internal context, that of the communication exchange itself, in which one utterance frames the next utterance and so on, as well as the external context, that of a telephone call from a user to the operating service.

Context has great influence on the language we use. A common remark is 'Yes but you don't ever say that, do you?' but it's not easy to state categorically that we *never* use a particular word or phrase – it will largely depend on the context.

Purpose

All speech performs a function: in speech we can make a promise or a threat, deliver a warning or rebuke, congratulate or apologise. Sometimes, this has to be stated explicitly: 'Are you going to bring me that book back?'/'Yes, I promise'; 'I've passed my test!'/ 'Congratulations!' Sometimes it's implicit in what we say (and understood in the context): 'You haven't put any sugar in it' = a complaint and request for sugar.

Receiver

The term 'receiver' needs a little attention. In any act of communication, other than talking to yourself or writing notes to yourself, there is a text producer and a text receiver. Speech is directed to *someone* rather than a vacuum. However, the word 'receiver' has been used to incorporate listeners and readers: it refers to the recipient of the text but all these terms, 'recipient', 'receiver', 'listener' and 'reader', are misleadingly passive.

The receiver, here the listener and co-speaker, has a very active role to play. In conversation, he or she helps to shape the discourse as it goes along, influencing what is said and how it's said. The receiver brings a certain amount of background knowledge to a text, interacts with the text, decodes it and interprets it in an individual way. However, we've so far avoided using the word 'participant', which is a commonly used word in speech activities because that can refer to the speaker too and at this point we want to focus primarily on the receiver.

Speaking, before any technological inventions, could only take place face-to-face. This meant that the receiver was always physically present. Today, of course, interaction can be displaced and the receiver can be any distance away but at least the voice has to be present.

Activity

Make a table with the following headings:

Activity	Context	Purpose	Receiver/s	Topic
private chat	walking home from the cinema	gossip	one good friend	the night before

What kinds of speaking activities did you take part in over the last few days? Fill in the details for yourself (the one here is given as an example). Consider the number of listeners, the relationship and whether they were physically present (or on the telephone). Then work in pairs and fill in the details for any other kinds of speaking activities you can think of but which haven't already been included in your lists. Discuss what aspects of the various components might affect the speech activity.

Commentary

Here are some of the aspects you need to consider:

◎ Participants – in any speech event, there's more than one participant. We can talk to one person or any number upwards, two to two hundred or more! Of course the nature of the activity will vary, as will the language used. We'll look at this in more detail in Unit 4. What other aspects of the nature of the participants, other than their number, affect communication?

◎ Degree of familiarity – how well do we know the participant/s?

◎ Age – are all members peers or is there any discrepancy? We'll speak quite differently to younger *and* older people *and* to people of the same age.

◎ Gender – conversations vary between members of the same sex, the opposite sex or mixed gender groups.

- ◎ Status – are there hierarchical positions, real or perceived, to consider?
- ◎ Shared background/cultural knowledge – are participants from the same geographical location, the same educational background, the same cultural background? Do they share knowledge of the events and topics being discussed?
- ◎ Activity type – what type of activities did you think of in your list? Were they all interactive? We tend to think of speech first and foremost in terms of conversation which in turn we think of as interactional (although we've all experienced trying to talk to someone who won't let us 'get a word in edgeways' and whose conversation bears more resemblance to a monologue). Most of us share broadly similar views of what talking is all about and we have certain expectations. But getting the balance of contribution just right can be a tricky business: if we're too brief, we risk being thought rude or brusque; if we say too much, we might be considered a talkative, insensitive bore.

Activity

If we discuss for a moment some of the words to do with 'speaking', we can reveal quite a lot about these expectations. Look at this set of words related to speech. What different meanings do they convey?

speak	*talk*	*lecture*	*gossip*	*chat*
dialogue	*monologue*	*discuss*	*tell*	*say*

Consider what difference a preposition can make:

talk to/with/at/about

or a suffix:

speaker   *talker*   *lecturer*

Commentary

We usually use the verb 'talk' to indicate a two-way conversation on a more or less equal footing but if we were to say, 'Boy, can she talk!' we probably mean she goes on a bit! If we say, 'He talked *at* me the whole time', we would probably mean we never a got a chance to say anything. This reveals that we have certain instincts about the nature and balance of participation in a conversation and when this is disturbed we might get annoyed or upset.

The nature of everyday speech

Most everyday speech is conversation. Remember that at this stage we're concentrating on what we *do* – we'll look at the language itself more closely in Unit 4. We'll take just a quick run-through here as other books in the *Intertext* series cover these aspects in more detail (*Working with Texts* (Unit 5) (Carter *et al.*, 2001), *The Language of Conversation* (Pridham, 2001)).

One short exchange between two participants will serve as an example of everyday speech interaction:

Conversation – Telephone enquiry to Greek Tourist Office

CALLER: I wondered if you had any free tourist literature on Rhodes
CLERK: yes
CALLER: er (2) um (2) could you (.) send me some please
CLERK: yes (1) your address

Conversation takes place in real time

Most everyday conversation is spontaneous, unplanned and un-rehearsed. It takes place in real time so we need to think on our feet. To give ourselves time to think, we often pause (represented by (2), (.), etc.) and hesitate ('er . . . um').

Conversation is face to face

Most conversations take place face to face (or voice to voice, over the phone, as here). Unlike writing, this allows us to get immediate feedback. Do our listeners understand us? Are they in agreement? Do they sympathise or empathise? Or not? We can judge many of these things from facial gestures, body language and of course our participants' verbal responses with their intonation. If necessary, we can change tack and use a different expression ('I wondered if you had' > 'could you send me').

Conversation has a purpose

The nature of this interaction is transactional. The purpose is very precise – action is required as an outcome of the conversation. However, some conversations are interpersonal with the purpose of, for example, establishing or maintaining a relationship.

Conversation is interactive

In order to interact, you need more than one person! The participants here don't know each other at all and so the language remains fairly formal and polite ('I wondered if'), with past tense use increasing the degree of politeness. The conversation involves turn-taking.

Turn-taking is such a basic, simple principle that it's an unconscious part of normal conversations. We take turns to say something in a conversation. A speaks first, then B responds, then A comes back. Here the caller initiates with requests and the clerk answers.

Whether we're speaking face-to-face or over the telephone, to one person or a small group, the wheels of conversation usually turn smoothly, with participants offering contributions at appropriate moments, with no undue gaps or, conversely, with everyone talking over each other. This is not to say that contributions always take place at precise intervals or that they're of equal length but with people of the same culture, the unspoken 'rules' of turn-taking are more or less followed and we tend to get disturbed if people, for one reason or another, don't play the game.

Here, although the exchange *is* authentic, it doesn't flow. The clerk's responses are so short that the caller feels lost. The clerk gives the impression, although presumably unintentionally, of being off-hand, uninterested and officious. The turn-taking isn't handled smoothly because the caller expects the clerk to take up the first turn and produce a longer, more effective turn in which action is offered. The discontinuation could be a result of cultural mismatch or personal mood (the clerk might indeed be fed up).

The pervasive nature of turn-taking in all kinds of human exchanges is often made explicit in various games, verbal or otherwise: consider board and card games that proceed systematically and are signalled with 'Your turn' or popular language games such as passing a familiar object for each person to make up a related saying, turn by turn. (A log of wood passed round a group, for example, provoked in one turn 'she's a chip off the old block' and ended with the final turn, 'I'm stumped!'.)

In games, we can be routine and predictable and 'even'. Turn-taking in conversation is, however, a normal part of human interaction and so the rules have to be more flexible. They can also be handled and signalled differently across different cultures, thus causing possible communication difficulties in conversations between people of different cultures and languages. In cross-linguistic exchanges, of course, even if turn-taking is successful, plain old misunderstandings can still occur. A TV street interviewer tries to tempt a passer-by to try a food test:

Are you peckish?
No, I'm Turkish.

Holding the floor

There may be particular occasions, in particular speech events, when turn-taking is either not the norm or it's not desirable. For example, the speaker might want to 'hold the floor'. The most obvious example is a political speech or a debate where the speaker doesn't want to be interrupted. But this can equally apply to teachers and lecturers (as well as the social bore)!

There are many techniques for doing this and some people are more skilful at it than others, either naturally or from training. It's difficult to interrupt someone who's speaking very fast, or who keeps the intonation raised, which signals they're continuing, rather than let it fall (the end of a phrase or clause . . .). If they don't signal a clear syntactic boundary (the end of phrase or clause, grammatically speaking), the other person can't break in. Voice pitch may be raised. Discourse markers, such as 'first', 'furthermore', make interrupting more difficult.

The phatic nature of conversation

A large and important part of conversation is **phatic talk**. That is, it has no concrete purpose other than to establish or maintain personal relationships. It's related to what is sometimes called small talk. Small talk, along with what has often been considered a British obsession of talking about the weather, has long been misunderstood. They both play an important social role in oiling the wheels of social intercourse. It tends to follow traditional patterns, with stock responses and formulaic expressions: 'How are you?'/'Fine' or, when talking about the weather, by capping the first speaker and exaggerating: 'Cold today, isn't it?'/'Freezing'. We tend not to question or deviate from these rituals. In fact, it's so unusual to do this that it's easily ridiculed:

'Good morning!' said Bilbo, and he meant it . . .

'What do you mean?' [Gandalf] said. 'Do you wish me a good morning, or mean that it is a good morning whether I want it or not; or that you feel good this morning; or that it is a morning to be good on?'

(Tolkien, 1966)

Activity

Either try this activity for yourself or ask a member of your family or a close friend to help you. You can either use a tape-recorder or just use your memory and make notes immediately.

Record the conversations you have over a period of time, such as a morning or an evening. Identify different features as outlined above. What percentage of the conversations would you categorise as 'phatic'? Did anything out of the ordinary happen?

To speak or not to speak

So far all the conversations have kept to fairly safe territory. Not many people would have a problem saying 'Good morning' but we *do* have options with communication, some of which we looked at in Unit 1. We don't just have the choice between writing and speaking; we can also choose to speak or stay silent; to speak at one given moment or another. One influential factor is that of 'face'.

Face

The concept of face is also covered in *Working with Texts* (Carter *et al.*, 2001) and *The Language of Conversation* (Pridham, 2001). We mention it here because it can affect what we do when we speak. Look at this next authentic conversation.

Teenage school-children who are walking down the road are overheard discussing lessons:

A: you'd never dream of asking the teacher t..to explain something
    in the middle of the lesson 'cos (.) everyone'd really HATE |you
B: |you'd wait till afterwards
    for a private wor|d
C: |you'd sound really thick (.) so embarrassing

29

Here the teenagers are concerned to protect their positive face – they want to be liked, not hated; they don't want to feel embarrassed. These factors influence *when* they choose to ask the question. Not that it's on record but it would no doubt affect the language chosen too. You often hear people preface questions with 'Can I ask a really thick/stupid question?' in order to save face and avoid being thought even more stupid . . . for failing to realise the question may be thought stupid! After class, you would more probably be concerned with the negative face – not wanting to impinge on others – and so might preface the question with 'Could I have a minute?'

Speaking isn't only conversation

So far we've only concentrated on the features which apply to interactional speech activities. Although conversation makes up the largest part of everyday oral communication, we also take part in less interactional, more one-way activities. We might have to give a talk in front of the class as part of a project; we might give oral instructions on how to repair something or cook something; we might give a lengthy narration of something exciting that happened to us. The language and style will then be different. It may need to be planned beforehand; it may be more formal; it may require a non-verbal response; it may involve lengthier and more complex utterances. We need to remember that not all speech is informal, brief and dependent on an active participant.

Accent

People often feel very strongly that language is part of their identity and one aspect of oral production which seems to reflect this more than any other is **accent** and **dialect**. Accent refers to the sound quality – the sounds of the individual **phonemes** – whereas dialect additionally covers particular use of lexis and grammar.

There is evidence to suggest that accents are subject to 'levelling' nowadays; that is, they are becoming less prominent and are merging, due to increased mobility. However, regional accents *do* still exist and are the subject of hot debate, often fiercely defended by their owners. In schools, there may well be a policy to advocate Standard English (be it Standard English English, American English, Australian English, etc.) and this can sometimes cause embarrassment or difficulty for someone with a prominent non-Standard accent.

Conclusion

Speech, in the context of everyday conversation, mostly does the following:

◎ takes place in real time;
◎ is conducted face-to-face;
◎ is interactional;
◎ consists of patterns and routines;
◎ follows certain principles.

In speech, we project our own personality and we construct and maintain personal and social relationships. We set out to achieve a particular purpose which might be interpersonal or transactional or both. We learn to adapt our language according to the various aspects of the context and, through experience, constantly develop strategies and learn new and appropriate language skills so that we can function more effectively in a growing number of new situations. In Unit 4, we'll see how these skills manifest themselves in terms of the actual language we use in speech.

Extension

1   Artificial intelligence is quite advanced today but very often it's still detectable as it's very difficult to reproduce natural-sounding speech by artificial means. Either make your own or find and re-record published recordings of: telephone announcements, computer-generated speech, artificial flight or rail announcements. You might also be able to find some examples of alien speech from old movies or television programmes. Analyse them in relation to the features listed on pp. 18–19 to see what features of natural speech are easier/more difficult to imitate.

2   Find a video-recording of a political speech or a TV debate. Write a commentary on the techniques of turn-taking and holding the floor used by the speakers.

3   Make a recording of speakers with different regional accents and a Standard accent (you could use a TV soap or a TV or radio chat programme). If possible, try to get a range of accents that aren't restricted to your own geographical area. Analyse the effects of the different accents on a) other characters in the programme, and b) on yourself and other listeners. Conduct a survey of family, friends and classmates to find out views on accents. Write up a report based on your findings.

The language of writing

The aim of this unit is to explore the language commonly used in written texts, both of a general and more specific nature. Think of all the hundreds of pieces of writing you see around you every day – a notice in a shop window, a restaurant menu, a shop receipt. As you walk along the street, you see many different types of written texts and they are, for the most part, instantly recognisable. When do you ever stop and think, 'I wonder what that is? Is it an advertising leaflet, a bill, a price list?' Not very often – and if you do, it's probably unusual in some way and we'll consider some peculiarities in Unit 6. So what is it that makes written texts so easy to recognise?

Activity

Nominate a few people in the group to collect together as many different written texts as they can (e.g. a newspaper article, phone bill, bank statement, driving licence). The 'volunteers' should then stand at the front of the room and quickly hold up one item at a time. See how quickly everyone manages to identify them. Now discuss what it is that makes these texts easy to recognise? Were there any texts which were not so easy to identify? If so, why was that?

Commentary

When studying language, it's easy to concentrate on the words alone and forget all the surrounding details which go into the creation of a text and become part of it. We can start with the smallest language unit, the word, (without going as small as a **morpheme** which is the smallest unit of *meaning* – see Index of terms for an example) and spiral outwards to larger and larger chunks of language: phrase, sentence, paragraph, whole text. But that's not the end of the story. From the activity, you found that there were more features *beyond* the language which helped to set the texts you were shown within a particular category or a specific genre.

How many of the following list did you mention before as affecting your ability to place the texts?

◎ Physical aspects: quality/size/colour of paper or card;
◎ Typographical features related to:

  ◎ printing: font size and style, formatting (bold, italics, etc.);
  ◎ layout: columns, continuous text or bulleted lists, etc., white space;
  ◎ positioning: headlines, captions, justified, centred or aligned text, etc.

◎ Graphics: photos, print images, cartoons, symbols.

Context

The most important thing to remember about any piece of communication is that it doesn't exist in a vacuum. It has been created, as we've already said, within a specific set of circumstances for a specific purpose and reflects many factors which have influenced its design, style, layout, structure and language. As readers, or even casual observers, we usually meet the text within its normal environment – the menu on a restaurant table, the electricity bill in an envelope on the doormat and so on – and therefore we bring to the text a great deal of background knowledge, predictions and expectations, which help us make sense of what we see. It's only when we meet a new kind of text which we have never experienced before (either because of a cultural change or a new technological invention – or when a text takes on an unfamiliar guise, such as political propaganda masquerading as an advert) that we need time to readjust our mindset in order to decode accurately the information in the text.

There are people working in many professions who know only too well how important these aspects are: graphic designers, desktop publishers, web-page designers, etc. These people devote as much attention to these features as they do to the printed word. But they're not the only ones who should consider their importance. They affect and influence all of us – as consumers, students, voters – and sometimes we can be manipulated, as readers, if we're not aware of some of the more subtle messages being conveyed. On the other side of the coin, as writers, we might convey the wrong kind of message if such features are applied inappropriately.

Effects on language

The relationship between supporting features and the language itself is very close – and it's a two-way relationship, i.e. (a) the visual image sets up expectations in the reader of what language to expect and (b) the features themselves are part of the language or part of the text in which the language appears and convey or reinforce the message. Consider these images as examples: the front cover of this book and the Text: Ice cream land (over the page).

Activity

Turn to the front cover of this book. What does the cover tell you?

Commentary

The words in the title communicate to the reader the subject content of the book itself but there are more than just words there. The images reinforce visually the subject matter contained in the book, covering both aspects of speech and writing in a modern context. More subtly, they convey a number of skills: speaker as listener, writer as reader. At first glance, you should get the impression of a factual book but not a heavy scholarly tome. Does it appeal to the intended audience? That's for you to decide.

Activity

Look at the Text: Ice cream land. What do the print fonts tell you?

Text: Ice cream land

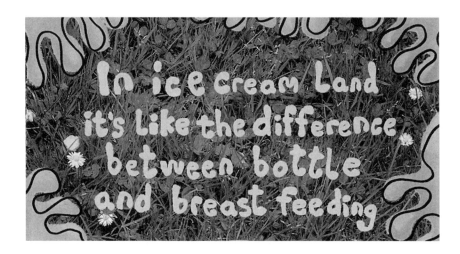

Commentary

In the text shown, such a print style with rounded lettering, replicating a child's unjoined-up handwriting, looks very childlike and, in addition, was originally printed in baby pink colouring. The font chosen reflects the desired image of the product and conveys the message of the ice cream being soft and smooth and appealing to children. This works alongside the language which with 'ice cream land' is reminiscent of fairy stories (so aimed at children) and with 'bottle and breast feeding' targets mothers.

Activity

Find some similar examples from newspapers and magazines. Analyse the message that is being conveyed and/or reinforced by the print font and style. Then convert the style to convey a different message, to promote perhaps a different product or a different aspect of the same product.

Activity

Look at the Text: Migraine advertisement. What do you think the effect of the font is?

Text: **Migraine advertisement**

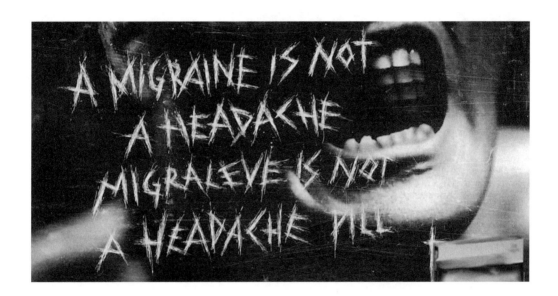

Commentary

Such sharp jagged lettering, this time in capitals, reflects the pain of a migraine attack and sets up topic associations. The font style is suggestive of searing pain and the resulting feeling of being out of control. In other contexts, capitalisation can be used to reflect emotion, such as in a novel to suggest anger 'I HATE YOU!' or to convey shouting and intensity, as in an email 'I DIDN'T MEAN IT'.

Activity

Look at these graphics and see the difference between the two uses of the bubbles. One is a thought bubble and the other is a speech bubble.

Commentary

The language we expect to read inside these images will be different. In the first, we expect to read language which is supposed to represent thought while in the second, we expect to read language intended to represent actual speech. So when we come across these in their actual contexts, we absorb the visual and verbal message in combination.

Look at the advert in the Text: Alfa Romeo and discuss its design. The ad is obviously based on another text type. What are the distinctive features of this other text? What assumptions does it make about the previous knowledge of the reader? Why has this format been chosen?

Text: Alfa Romeo

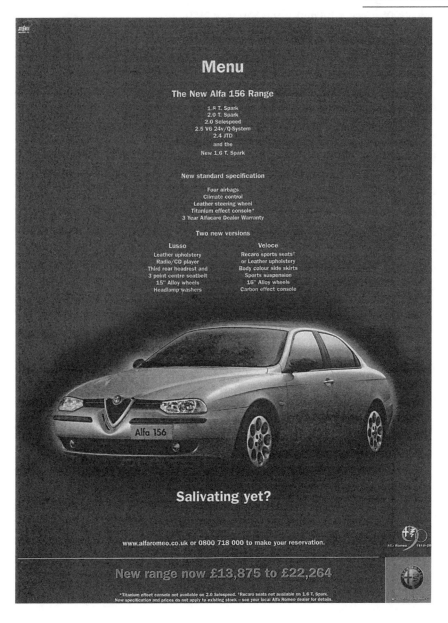

Commentary

The ad is eye-catching. The menu format is very familiar but strikes us even more forcibly, being taken so completely out of context. Even without the word 'Menu' at the top, the layout is so conventional that it is instantly recognisable, with the wording centred on the page and the positioning of the text such as to represent the different courses and options of a meal. It therefore assumes our knowledge of such texts and such formats. 'Salivating' is obviously connected to eating and so the ad works on a very sensuous level, appealing to a sophisticated consumer.

How often do we get as far as studying a menu in a restaurant and then walk out? Not very often. The ad is therefore based on an underlying assumption that we *will* choose, i.e. buy, this car. It takes for granted our interest and desire and reinforces ideas of individual taste, choice and satisfaction.

Genre

So far the focus has been more on the supporting evidence and non-linguistic elements but of course *what* they support, the language itself, is of prime importance. Continuous language forms texts which belong to a genre. They will therefore share certain features but they're not absolutely identical.

Taking one example of a common genre to start with, letter-writing is one in which everyone is involved at some point or another. But if someone told you to 'write a letter', would you know precisely what to write? There are so many different types of letters which vary according to the factors related to CPR, see below:

		C – introductory, one of a series, reply
	personal	P – chat, invite, thank, express sympathy
		R – friend, relative
Letter		
		C – response to ad, office report
	formal	P – complain, request, inform
		R – customer, company, employer

We could go on and on. What this means is that any one genre could be divided into sub-genres. In each case, the language will be affected. Even within the same sub-genre, texts are rarely identical.

Activity

Here are two examples of a letter of complaint from a private consumer to a large company. With similar CPRs, you would expect the letters to be very similar but is this in fact the case? Draw up a list of the similarities and differences.

Text: Ellie's letter

34 Newtown Drive
Ellington, Newtown.
NNX 4NT
Telephone 01273 621 331

13th February, 2000

Dear Sir,

When I opened my toffee crunch corner I was really surprised to see that there weren't any chocolate rings in there. Please can you make sure you put some chocolate rings in next time.

"DON'T FORGET"

Yours faithfully

Ellie Miller
Age 7

Text: Sue's letter

82 Main Street
Overton
Newtown
NN5 4PG
Tel/Fax: 01273 271 544
e-mail: suesimner@hotline.com

Customer Services   20 April 2000
Thorntons plc
Thornton Park
Alfreton
Derbyshire
DE55 4XJ

Dear Sirs

Amazing to find, difficult to believe, impossible to prove! But the bag of biscuits, as enclosed, contained not 5 but only 4 biscuits!!

I recently bought this packet from your store in the McArthur Glen outlet centre, near the M1 motorway in Derbyshire. I've bought these biscuits many times before and never had any problems whatsoever, and the products have always been delicious. So you can imagine my surprise and my disappointment when I opened this packet!

I would be very interested to hear how such a thing could have happened and I look forward to receiving your explanation.

With thanks in advance.

Yours faithfully

Sue Simner

Commentary

There are certain similarities: first of all, most basically, they are both written texts, employing graphological methods and various writing sub-skills, as outlined earlier. They both follow the conventions of formal letter-writing by placing the date and the writer's address at the top (though positioning varies); both use formulaic expressions for the opening greetings and closings. In both, we can find complex sentence constructions ('When I opened . . . I was really surprised'; 'So you can imagine . . . when I opened'). In both, there are features reflecting the permanent, formal, uni-directional nature of writing described already. Functionally, both letters describe the problem and the feeling it provoked and anticipate future action on the part of the receiver. But then the most striking variation comes in style, with the first being very direct ('Please can you make sure you put some chocolate rings in next time. "DON'T FORGET"') and the other taking a more indirect approach ('I would be very interested to hear . . .'). At this point, the letters diverge, with the first veering towards closer resemblance to spoken language – note the use of capitals as highlighted before and quotation marks – while the second letter stays firmly rooted in written mode.

The implication is that something needs to be added to our frame-work. CPR is not sufficient. We have to consider the person who creates the message, thus giving us:

Context   **P**urpose   **P**roducer   **R**eceiver

Various factors related to the producer of the message will also affect the language: age, gender, personality, educational background, intellect, **idiolect** (see Unit 5), status, individual creativity, and so on. This gives us an infinite variety of texts in any language, both written and spoken.

Activity

Now look at the two replies to the above letters. Compare the similarities and differences and discuss the reasons for them.

Text: Müller's reply

MÜLLER DAIRY (UK) LIMITED
Shrewsbury Road,
Market Drayton,
Shropshire, TF9 3SQ
Tel: 01630 960202
Fax: 01630 960203

C/001/593/MG/1
WITHOUT PREJUDICE

17th February 2000

Miss E Miller
34 Newtown
Ellington
NEWTOWN
NNX 4NT

Dear Miss Miller

We were most concerned to learn of your complaint regarding one of our products and full details have been given to our Quality Assurance Department.

We appreciate the time you have taken to bring this to our attention and would like you to accept as a gesture of the Company's goodwill, the enclosed reimbursement, with the hope that you have no further problems with our products.

Yours sincerely

Miss M. Gates
Customer Relations Assistant

Enc. Voucher £3.00

Text: Thorntons' reply

THORNTONS PLC
Thornton Park, Somercotes,
Alfreton, Derbyshire DE55 4XJ
Telephone 01773 455341
Fax 01773 455961
Directors Fax 01773 455724

HW/VT/053942

16 May 2000

Ms S Simner
82 Main Street
Overton
Newtown
NN5 4PG

Dear Ms Simner

I was most concerned to learn from your letter that the bag of Apricot 'n' Almond Choccies that you purchased from our McArthur Glen store recently contained four Choccies and not five.

I do hope you will accept my sincere apologises on behalf of the Company for your disappointment with your purchase on this occasion. Please be assured I have bought this to the attention of both our production and packaging teams and also the product manager who looks after our Choccies range. It would appear that this is due to an error during the packaging process. Please be assured that all products are checked weighed before despatch and any underweight products are normally rejected. Steps are being taken to ensure this does not recur again.

Thank you for taking the time and trouble to bring this matter to our attention. In order that you may purchase replacement confectionary I have enclosed some gift vouchers, I do hope you will use these with my compliments, next time you visit one of our stores.

I do hope that we may continue to be of service to you in the future.

Yours sincerely

Vanessa Taylor (Mrs)
Customer Services Department

Enc: £2.00 Voucher

Commentary

Taking the functions first of all, similar functions are expressed. Both express concern to hear of the problem – both in the superlative ('most concerned'). Both express appreciation at being alerted to the problem ('We appreciate the time', 'Thank you for taking the time . . .'). Both aim at appeasement by taking the action of offering reimbursement (sending vouchers). Both follow similar conventions of address and greetings formulae, although you can notice slight differences. The main difference is the length, due to the inclusion in the Thorntons letter of an explanation as to the likely cause, whilst no explanation is offered in the Müller letter. Possibly the writer takes the age of the receiver into account whilst noticeably *not* talking down. (Müller, interestingly, deems it necessary to include **WITHOUT PREJUDICE** at the top, which is a stock, legalistic phrase, implying that the company is not admitting to any fault on their part.)

Genre expectations

Many texts within the same genre follow similar patterns of layout, style and language. Most people within a Westernised culture share a pretty fixed idea of what a recipe genre, for example, involves; we could even say we hold a stereotypical view of a recipe. But do all recipes convey identical messages? Are all recipes produced within the same context? Do they all have the same purpose? Do they all have the same target readership?

Activity

Without referring to any actual examples, invent your own recipe. It could be for your favourite dish or totally fantastical: you could invent new ingredients and new methods for an alien visitor, a mountain trek, whatever you like. Indicate whether it's designed as a one-off recipe or to fit a particular publication. You can develop this with graphics if you like but the main aim at this stage is to focus on the language. Compare the similarities and differences of the various versions.

Commentary

- ◎ Language – Did you use stock phrases or formulaic expressions? What vocabulary was specific to cooking? Did any 'unusual' features appear?
- ◎ Grammar – What was the grammar of the instructions – imperatives ('add', 'stir'), address to the reader ('you take . . .'), full sentences or note form?
- ◎ Conventions – Did you use abbreviations for weights and measures? Were these existing ones or did you invent your own, and, if so, were they recognisable and consistent throughout the recipe?
- ◎ Layout – Did you start with a list of ingredients and then go on to give instructions? What about the use of columns versus paragraphs?
- ◎ Readership – How is the intended readership reflected in the text?
- ◎ Context – How is the context reflected in the text?

Activity

Three recipes follow. The genre, then, is the same but the recipes are far from identical. Look at:

Context (**C**)   Purpose (**P**)   Producer (**P**)   Receiver (**R**)

By considering CPPR, we can see what the writer is trying to communicate and the direct effects on the language used in each case, in terms of grammar and vocabulary.

Text: Sloppy Joes

Sloppy Joes

A good way to utilize a little bit of raw hamburger that's mighty popular with the young set.

½ lb. ground beef	⅓ bottle chili sauce
1 tablesp. butter	1½ tablesps. brown sugar
½ cup chopped onion	1 teasp. Worcestershire sauce
⅓ cup chopped celery	2 teasps. vinegar
3 tablesps. chopped green pepper	½ teasp. salt

Brown meat in butter; add onion, celery and green pepper. Cook slowly until tender but not brown. Add other ingredients and simmer 20 minutes. Serve on 6 toasted hamburger buns with potato chips, relishes, and cokes.

Commentary

We get a lot of clues as to context from the language itself which in turn is greatly influenced by the context. This recipe comes from a little book which aims 'to take the stigma out of "leftovers"' and 'to help you have fun' with them. Hence, this recipe, as with all the others in the book, is introduced by stating its purpose and offering a suggestion to the cook. The word 'utilize', meaning to make use of (existing ingredients rather than buying fresh ingredients), reinforces the stated aims of the book.

There are many words which indicate the origins of time and place: some of the ingredients ('raw hamburger', 'hamburger buns', 'potato chips') were particularly coming to the fore in the mid-1960s but would be unlikely to appear in a British recipe book, for example, until some time later. The dish name, Sloppy Joes, and the expression 'mighty popular' indicate the American origin.

Otherwise the format is fairly standard:

- list of ingredients in a familiar two-column layout;
- measurements in figures with standard abbreviations ('lb.', 'teasp.', 'tablesps.');
- instructions in the imperative form ('Brown', 'add', 'cook', 'serve');
- short sentences omitting grammar items such as

  - articles ('Brown [the] meat', 'add [the] onion');
  - pronouns with verb 'to be' ('Cook slowly until [they're] tender');
  - prepositions ('simmer [for] 20 minutes').

The recipe is short, simple and easy to follow which is again fitting for a 'leftovers' recipe book where the cook wants to get straight down to the job.

Activity

Look at the Text: Toulouse sausage cassoulet and consider its CPPR.

Text: Toulouse Sausage Cassoulet

Meat

INGREDIENTS
1 pack Toulouse Sausages
1 tablespoon olive oil
250g bag shallots, peeled
1 clove garlic, crushed
400g can chopped
tomatoes
300ml (½ pint) red wine
150ml (¼ pint) stock
420g can cannellini beans
400g can flageolet beans
1 teaspoon cornflour,
blended in a little cold water
1 tablespoon freshly
chopped thyme
salt and freshly ground
black pepper

TOULOUSE SAUSAGE CASSOULET

PREPARATION TIME: 10 MINUTES   **COOKING TIME:** 20 MINUTES

Sainsbury's Toulouse Sausages are made to a French recipe using coarsely chopped pork. They are the traditional ingredient in *cassoulet* – a rich, herby sausage and bean stew.

1 Cook the sausages following pack instructions.
2 Meanwhile, heat the oil in a flameproof casserole and brown the shallots on all sides. Stir in the garlic and cook for a further minute.

3 Slice each sausage into 3 diagonally and add to the casserole with the tomatoes, wine, stock and beans. Bring to the boil and simmer gently for 10 minutes. (Alternatively, bake in a preheated oven at 200°C, 400°F, Gas Mark 6 for 15 minutes.)
4 Stir in the blended cornflour, most of the thyme and seasoning to taste. Cook for a further 5 minutes and serve sprinkled with the remaining chopped thyme.

SERVES: 3-4
PER SERVING: 742 calories; 45g fat

BRITISH
MEAT
Pork

WINE SUGGESTION:
Sainsbury's Cahors

Sainsbury's

FRESH FOOD, FRESH IDEAS.

For other original recipes, visit Sainsbury's website at www.sainsburys.co.uk

SAINSBURY'S SUPERMARKETS LTD, STAMFORD STREET LONDON SE1 9LL
All items subject to availability. Some items available in larger stores only. 729/828 NCC

49

Commentary

This has a similar, fairly standard layout. It's more modern in appearance and physical format (the original being produced on glossy, semi-rigid card) with colour photos and coloured text background. It refers to modern packs, cans and gram measurements (as opposed to imperial measurements in earlier British contexts). It has straightforward step by step, numbered instructions.

But the purpose is not solely to inform and pass on culinary expertise; this is a recipe card produced by a supermarket to increase sales by forming a direct link between the purchase and the cooking. It needs to appeal to the busy, modern cook who will be attracted by the following:

◎ simple language of instruction ('Slice each sausage into 3 diagonally');
◎ language related to nutritional value ('PER SERVING: 742 calories; 45g fat') and healthy eating ('<u>freshly</u> chopped thyme', '<u>freshly</u> ground black pepper');
◎ speed of preparation and cooking time ('PREPARATION TIME: 10 MINUTES COOKING TIME: 20 MINUTES');
◎ clear presentation.

Simple imperatives are used for the instructions ('Cook', 'heat', 'brown', 'simmer') but it was presumably felt it would be clearer if written grammatically, without any omissions ('Stir in <u>the</u> blended cornflour, most of <u>the</u> thyme <u>and</u> seasoning to taste'). Using a French word for the name of the dish (*cassoulet*) as opposed to the standard English 'casserole' (incidentally of French origin too) adds a touch of exotica to appeal to the consumer.

Many of the words used, obviously, are typical of cookery writing:

◎ verbs related to food preparation ('add', 'cook', 'serve', 'brown', 'bake');
◎ typical adjectives to describe the processed ingredients ('peeled', 'chopped', 'crushed', 'ground', 'blended', 'sprinkled');
◎ nouns referring to cookery equipment ('flameproof casserole', 'preheated oven');
◎ phrases of cooking methods ('seasoning to taste', 'bring to the boil', 'simmer gently', 'cook for a further').

Activity

Look at the Text: Oysters and sausages and consider CPPR again.

Text: Oysters and sausages

Fry some chipolata sausages.
Serve them very hot on a dish and on a second dish a dozen oysters.
Alternate the sensations.
Burn your mouth with a crackling sausage.
Soothe your burns with a cool oyster.
Continue until all the sausages and oysters have disappeared.

White wine, of course.

Commentary

This is more about the eating experience than the cooking – and a sensuous one at that. Here it's not so important to be precise ('some chipolata sausages'). It imitates a conventional recipe with the instructional format using imperative verbs ('Fry', 'Burn') so that it's almost a parody. Although the high-class ingredients are obviously aimed at a sophisticated connoisseur, interestingly the ingredients of the Toulouse sausage recipe are not very different, in that case reflecting the desire to attract the shopper who aspires to a higher-class eating experience.

However, artistically the verbs move away from normal recipe instructional verbs ('Alternate', 'soothe') and the adjectives are very noticeable in their sense appeal and contrast ('crackling', 'cool').

Table 3.1 The CPPR of the three recipes

Context	Purpose	Producer	Receiver
recipe book mid-1960s	to instruct how to use up leftovers	professional chef	American parent with financial concerns
supermarket recipe card – free handout	to give cooking instructions; to promote sales	supermarket chain	busy shopper – health conscious; more exotic tastes than 'bangers and mash'!
cookery book	to convey the joys of an eating experience	Doctor Edouard de Pomiane – nineteenth century food writer	sophisticated cook

Activity

Have a look at this description of a Burger King Whopper. It's full of adjectives and adverbs.

Whopper

Toasted sesame seed bun. Fresh crisp lettuce. Tasty ketchup.

Crunchy pickles. Creamy mayonnaise. Ripe red tomatoes.

Freshly cut onions. Flame-grilled beef patty.

Imagine you've been asked to write an encyclopaedic entry for this. Re-write the above in full sentences, making it purely factual. What has happened to the adjectives/adverbs and why?

Commentary

You should have found that many of the adjectives and adverbs were removed or altered. Why? Some adjectives in the original are totally factual, describing real-world, indisputable items. The bun, for example, *is* toasted and contains sesame seeds. This could be proven in a court of law, if necessary. You could, therefore, have kept that in. At the other end of the spectrum is 'tasty'. That's arguable. Someone might find the ketchup bland. 'Tasty' also implies positive values, i.e. having a nice taste, but some people might not like it. You probably removed 'tasty' or changed it to fact, e.g. 'tomato'. 'Crunchy' and 'creamy' could indeed be valid but they've been selected less for their truth value than for their sense appeal. Even 'flame-grilled', while factual, evokes connotations of natural, outdoor barbecue cooking and sounds attractive. What at first sight seems quite a straightforward description is in fact overloaded with images to attract and manipulate the consumer, in differing degrees.

Activity

Look at these extracts from everyday texts. Can you recognise where they come from?

Text: Specialised language

DO NOT EXCEED THE STATED DOSE
If symptoms persist, consult your doctor.

*Finely chopped,
roasted hazelnuts blended
with smooth praline*

THIS AGREEMENT MADE THE   DAY OF
between . . . .
of . . . .
(hereinafter called the Landlord) of the one part
and . . . .
of . . . .
(hereinafter called the Tenant) of the other part.

SECTION A to be completed by **Applicant** in black ink
using BLOCK LETTERS

*A failure on the part of a person to observe any provision of **The Highway Code** shall not of itself render that person liable to criminal proceedings of any kind, but any such failure may in any proceedings (whether civil or criminal . . .) be relied upon by any party to the proceedings as tending to establish or negative any liability which is in question in those proceedings.*

Can you help your dog look and feel healthier by what you feed him?

2. I/We have read and fully understand the terms and conditions comprised in part 11 of this agreement overleaf.

**'Cuts through the hype and makes all others look
like nerdy textbooks'**
The Australian

53

Commentary

You shouldn't have had much difficulty in generally recognising these texts. We meet many texts every day which we may need to read and make sense of but which we won't normally be required to produce ourselves. They tend to be related to specific contexts and certain professions – legal, medical, academic, journalism – and we usually have enough linguistic knowledge to make at least a rough stab at understanding them. Alternatively, we can seek expert help or look in a dictionary. We pick up a lot of rudimentary knowledge passively, particularly impressed on us by the force of the media, although if the need did arise for us to produce an accurate version of such a text, we might need to get expert training.

Language of specialised writing

A group of students recently demonstrated how much they'd absorbed from 'cop' programmes when asked to turn the children's verse 'Incey Wincey Spider' into a written police statement as read out in court. Here is the original verse followed by one student's version:

> Incey wincey spider
> Climbed the water spout.
> Down came the rain
> And washed poor spider out.
> Out came the sun
> And dried up all the rain.
> Incey wincey spider
> Climbed the spout again.

```
The here accused spider was witnessed climbing the
aforementioned drainage system. At 3 p.m. it began
to downpour which therefore led to the subsequent
expulsion from said drainpipe. At 3.15 precisely,
the rain ceased giving the accused the opportunity
to re-ascend.
```

Never mind how faithfully accurate this is or is not. The point is that it *seems* right. What's going on here? The original, a children's verse, has end-line rhyme, is mostly monosyllabic and sounds childlike with the name, Incey wincey, which not only rhymes but has the diminutive -y ending (like *doggy, bunny*). The sentences are single clauses or involve simple co-ordination ('and'). It is simple entertainment, written to accompany basic actions, such as finger climbing and tickling.

The police report is written to convey facts with absolute clarity. It is detailed and precise and logically sequenced.

The vocabulary, grammar, register all fit the text:

- vocabulary – legal **lexis** ('accused', 'witnessed', 'aforementioned', 'subsequent', 'said');
- grammar – piling up of adjectives before nouns, often formed from verb participles: ('here accused spider', 'aforementioned drainage system'); impersonal structures: passive ('was witnessed'), impersonal causal agent ('the rain ceased giving . . .');
- the writer has invented 'downpour' as a verb, which only exists in noun form in standard English, presumably because it seemed to fit the formal tone;
- register – vocabulary and grammar combine with factual precision, front positioning in the sentence of time elements ('At 3 p.m.', 'At 3.15 precisely') and formality ('ceased', 're-ascend') to produce the expected register of a (stereo)typical police statement.

Activity

Analyse the earlier examples of specialised language (p. 53) in a similar way. Try to find some more examples of language from other sources (business, media, science) which seem representative and analyse them contrastively. Pick out the features which seem characteristic of, for example, legal, medical or advertising language.

Commentary

Some features, from the texts on p. 53, listed in Table 3.2 (over) might help in the analysis of the texts you've found yourselves. They are not exhaustive but just serve as brief examples.

Table 3.2 Features of specialised language

Language area	Lexis	Grammar	Style
medical	'dose', 'symptoms', 'doctor'	negative imperative 'Do not exceed'	clear, formal
advertising	'blended', 'smooth' 'help your dog'	adjective descriptions 'finely chopped' direct question 'Can you help?'	persuasive, appealing to senses or to moral obligation
official	'section A', 'applicant', 'block letters', 'comprised', 'overleaf'	passive 'to be completed' reduced clauses 'comprised in'	formal, impersonal, unambiguous
book review	no particular lexis in this example related to book reviews but layout and punctuation convey the context; lexis-related style	ellipsis 'cuts through . . . all others' (= all other similar books)	colloquial, modern 'hype', 'nerdy'

Conclusion

In this unit, we've looked at the various features which surround the language of written texts and which are very much a part of the text. We've also studied the effect of these on language.

Taking CPPR as a framework, we've seen the effect on language in terms of:

◎ lexis
◎ grammar
◎ style

and seen how these relate in detail to both general texts and more specific texts, such as those produced in the field of law, medicine and advertising.

Extension

1 Divide into groups of about four or five. Each group should decide on a chosen text type: a blurb for the back page of a popular novel, a cereal packet competition, a school event poster, etc. (The groups

should *not* reveal to the other groups what they have chosen.) Each member of the group then goes away and produces an independent version of the chosen text type. Concentrate on the *appearance* as well as the language.

Re-form your groups and compare your versions. Discuss the details which are noticeably similar and different.

Ask the teacher to display them at random around the room. It's not a competition to find 'the best one' but to see how much leeway for individuality there is within a certain field and/or how much the text type determines the use of such features as outlined above.

You should then walk round the room and see if you can identify texts of the same type in order to collect them together.

2   Use the texts again that you produced for the first extension exercise but now concentrate on the language. Within each text type, identify any similar language produced by the different authors. In what ways did they differ? Were there any overlaps across the different genres? Do you think that some words or expressions were inappropriate and, if so, how could they be improved? Write a detailed commentary, with examples, on your findings.

3   Everyone should write on a piece of paper a written text type (e.g. popular press front page article, science experiment write-up). Collect all the papers and distribute them at random. Convert 'Incey Wincey Spider' (or any other well-known verse or song) into the stated written register. (Versions could later be read aloud to see if other members of the group can identify the imitated genre.)

The language of speaking

The aim of this unit is to identify commonly occurring features of everyday spoken English. This unit picks up the aspects identified in Unit 2 where we said that speaking, in everyday conversation, usually does the following:

- ◎ takes place in real time;
- ◎ is conducted face-to-face;
- ◎ is interactional.

Now if we see what these mean in terms of language, in relation to all of these we can focus on language features within three broad categories:

- ◎ grammar;
- ◎ lexis;
- ◎ discourse.

What we *achieve* when we speak is explored in the final part of this unit.

Look at the Text: Doing a job. This is an extended exchange between four participants and it illustrates many of the features common to everyday conversation. In relation to CPPR, all the speakers are friends or relatives. Speaker 1 is Speaker 2's niece; Speaker 3 is Speaker 1's wife; Speaker 4 is Speaker 2's partner. It takes place in the informal setting of Speaker 2's bedroom in the house where Speakers 1 and 3 are staying for the weekend with their baby. It's probably difficult to work out exactly what they're all talking about but the purpose seems to be to work together to assemble something, according to written instructions. What do you think they are doing? What features appear to be related to spoken language?

Text: Doing a job

```
 1 <S 01>   it should fit there cos it's not that big I don't think
 2 [7 secs]
 3 <S 02>   it's warm in here shall I turn that down?
 4 <S 01>   we've got the instructions anyway
 5 [8 secs]
 6 <S 03>   just put it by the
 7          window or something
 8 [4 secs]
 9 <S 04>   d'you want me to take that?
10 [4 secs]
11 <S 02>   ooh . . . then there's bedding for about ten people here
12 [laughs]
13 [12 secs]
14 <S 04>   ah
15 <S 01>   oh I say, ah we've got some more instructions
16 [12 secs]
17 <S 01>   that bit there's the bottom
18 <S 02>   d'you know you went up to erm Nottingham yesterday and
19          you still didn't take Roger's duvet
20 <S 04>   well . . . I wouldn't have had time to take it in any
21          case, haven't seen him
22 <S 02>   does he know we've got it?
23 <S 04>   no . . . oh look at that
24 <S 02>   it's not [inaudible]
25 <S 03>   it's not as difficult as it first seemed
26 <S 01>   she says you've got to twist these round and it makes
27          them solid or something
28 <S 03>   and all this just for you [<S 02> oh [laughs]]
29 <S 01>   there that's solid now
30 <S 02>   I think I've made it unsolid sorry I've done it the
31          wrong way round have I
32 [3 secs]
33 <S 01>   solid
34 [4 secs]
35 <S 03>   [laughs] [inaudible]
36 <S 01>   right now it's your end now
37 <S 02>   oh I see right okay
```

Commentary

In fact, they're busy trying to assemble a portable cot. Some of the features you may have noticed relate to situational factors:

◎ Face to face – The speakers are all face to face, sharing the same 'here and now'. This allows them to make constant reference to things around them which all speakers can understand and know what is being referred to. The language accompanies action so speakers give others instructions and silence indicates ongoing action. Relationships are reinforced with shared laughter.

◎ Interactional – The speakers interact with each other constantly – questions are answered, instructions are acted upon and agreement is expressed.

◎ Real time – Just as language prompts action, action prompts language and the two proceed as time goes on, at the moment of happening. Responses are unplanned and spontaneous and the speakers think on their feet, producing language which reflects this. We often start to say something and change our mind midway ('there . . . what's that in the middle'), which is termed a false start. We also add fairly meaningless words to fill the gaps, thus called **fillers** ('well') and these are prefabricated, highly conventional words and phrases in a language. Obviously, to give ourselves time to think, we frequently pause, as indicated by the bracketed figures in seconds, and express sounds of hesitation ('erm').

Grammar

Other features are directly related to language.

When we speak, we don't normally have time to work out long complex sentences with embedded clauses. We tend, therefore, to speak in short stretches which may or may not be accurate or complete sentences. This is why the term 'utterance' is preferred instead of 'sentence', as explained in the Introduction. In fact, much of what we say is broken, incomplete, fragmented segments ('solid', 'no too much', 'oh it's . . .'). If we do link these segments together, we tend to keep to simple linking devices, usually of co-ordination – 'and', 'but', 'or' ('you've got to twist these round and it makes them solid or something').

Word order normally follows conventional patterns (Subject Verb Object) (SVO) but there are times when variation serves our purpose better. We might want to stress a contrast and thus **front** the object, giving us an OSV pattern, e.g. 'This one I'm keeping; that one I'm taking back'.

Very common in spoken English, and very rare in writing, is topic fronting where a noun (or noun phrase or noun clause) is placed at the front before the grammatical subject, both of which in fact refer to the same thing: 'that bit there's the bottom.' We often save time in speaking by cutting down on language where possible, by using contractions ('didn't', 'you've') and **ellipsis**. This is where redundant words, which aren't strictly needed to convey the message, aren't uttered ('and all this [is] just for you', 'you've got to twist these [pieces/legs] round', 'no [that's] too much'). The former and latter are examples of omitted grammatical words where the sense conveyed by the verb is supplied by the larger segment but the middle example is an omitted lexical item where the sense is conveyed by the presence of the object in full sight of the speakers. This is also an example of **deixis**. When words, and pronouns feature frequently here, refer to something beyond the language of the text, they are described as deictic. Deixis is a feature much more common in speaking than in writing (except where texts make direct reference to objects, such as instruction manuals). It's also used to orient the conversation, not only in relation to the ongoing activity itself but also according to the participant's (one or all) perspective in terms of time ('yesterday' which only makes sense related to present time) or place ('you went up to Nottingham' where 'go up' frequently implies northwards). Orienting the listener is also the purpose behind topic fronting, so that the speaker can make sure the listener is clear what is being talked about before going any further ('that bit there').

Activity

Video or tape record a live commentary (sports or public news event) and transcribe a short section, highlighting any deictic terms you can find.

Lexis

We tend to use simple words based on Anglo-Saxon origins rather than complex vocabulary of French or Latin origin, e.g. start as opposed to commence. This is directly related to informality too. We would therefore normally keep to core vocabulary, the central words in a language – small, happy, dress – rather than spend time searching for words at the extreme ends of the language spectrum – minuscule, ecstatic, robe.

This is a huge generalisation as, of course, there are times when restricted core vocabulary simply doesn't convey the right meaning and when minuscule, ecstatic, robe are precisely the words needed. Context, again, is a vital factor. We might think that one verb of movement, for example, is perfectly adequate but when, for example, a lighting technician is giving instructions to an apprentice up a ladder, several are pressed into service in the course of this single utterance: 'you hook and slide; press it in; they glide and roll, turn and twitch.'

On the whole, however, spoken English has a lower lexical density than written English, using more grammar words and more verb phrases than noun phrases. Many of these verb phrases are based on the most common verbs in the language – go, have, put, do, etc. – which combine with nouns to make common phrases – go for a walk, have a wash, do the shopping. These are known as **delexical verbs** and are a common feature of informal spoken discourse.

In the text under discussion, there are hardly any real lexical words but many basic verbs, reflecting the activity which, if you haven't worked it out yet, is assembling a portable cot for the baby (put, make, done).

Many noun phrases make use of general words rather than specific or highly technical words ('that bit', 'the bottom'). This again relates to informality and shared knowledge between participants but purposes vary: to be all-encompassing, to be dismissive or humorous or to save time remembering the precise word for something. All sorts of words have been invented for this very common dilemma where we've forgotten – or we don't know – the name of something, such as thingumajig, thingumabob, what-you-may-call-it, doodah. This is related to **vague language** – a feature of spoken language identified and researched only relatively recently. This downplays precision and refers to objects and events in general terms. Common expressions or pronouns are tagged on at the end ('by the window or something', 'makes them solid or something') or might precede amounts if we're uncertain or don't want to sound too particular ('for about ten people', 'some more instructions').

Activity

In groups of four, two people role-play a conversation in pairs – in a shop, in the kitchen – in which no specific nouns can be used. General words and vague language have to predominate. The other two people observe and make notes.

Note all the general words and vague language you hear, putting an asterisk by any which couldn't be interpreted. 'Translate' the other expressions and check afterwards with the role-players if that's what they intended.

Lexical creativity

When studying language, it's easy to take broad categories and come up with a very uniform picture. It seems we all do the same things with oral communication, function in the same way and produce the same language. But of course, that's far from the truth – and it's what makes artificial intelligence language, however sophisticated nowadays, still sound *artificial*.

Every individual has his or her own idiolect – an individual way of using language, favourite words and expressions and so on (right, you know, to be honest). TV scriptwriters know this only too well, or at least discover it in the course of a series of a programmes, and capitalise on it with expressions which become their characters' catch phrases (I don't believe it, lovely-jubbly, OH MY GOD). Nothing reflects individuality as much as originality and every language user, to some extent or another, not only trots out tried and tested phrases but manages to be creative too.

At one time, it was thought you had to be a literary genius to create new words or new expressions (a Shakespeare, turning nouns into verbs: '*Grace* me no grace, nor *uncle* me no uncle', *Richard II*, II.iii.8; 'Doubly *portcullised* with my teeth and lips', ibid., I.iii.160). But creativity seems to be part of everyday human language use, as we explore, extend and play with existing words and meanings.

'Unsolid' ('Doing a job', p. 60, line 30) is not a standard word which could be found in a dictionary – and yet the dictionary is full of similar words which may well have started life in the same way. Whether words catch on and become common currency is down to many factors but inventiveness can only communicate if it's understandable – and that means it has to follow established conventions. Here, the standard adjective 'solid' has been taken as the root and the common prefix 'un' added to imply an opposite or a negative (as in 'undesirable'). So, although it's a creative and original lexical item, it's based on principled language rules.

Discourse

Conversation is interactive, therefore language which is used by one speaker, in one turn, directly affects the language in the next turn. It's quite wrong to take naturally occurring speech and isolate utterances because a great deal of the language interrelates and interweaves across longer stretches of the exchange. **Adjacency pairs** are not only fixed formulaic exchanges like 'Good morning'/'Good morning', but can be prompts and responses, as with questions and answers. A straight-forward example occurs here with 'does he know we've got it?'/'No' (lines 22–3). In the opening section though, we have the first part, the question 'shall I turn that down?', functioning as a suggestion or a kind of request for permission but the second part, the response, doesn't feature. If we'd been present at the time, maybe we would have seen gestures such as a nod, or a facial expression of a grin or simply an action taking place. The question could have been ignored. Whatever the reason, two-part exchanges might not always go as planned.

As we interact in conversation, we continually give signals of reinforcement and encouragement. These **back-channel** signs indicate that we're paying attention, that we're interested, in agreement and so on. Turns don't normally stop for them – they tend to slide into the conversation and overlap the turns. In English, the words most frequently used are yeah, right, OK, mmm and, although they seem rather insignificant, we soon realise how vital they are when they're missing. The totally silent listener will soon cause even the least sensitive speaker to stop talking, who is likely to infer lack of interest or sympathy. That is unless, as here, actions take the place of language so we don't find too many examples other than the occasional 'oh' and 'ah' which may also be conveying emotions.

Other signals are needed to indicate that a turn has ended or that a suitable juncture has been reached for interruption or interaction. **Discourse markers** mark the beginning of a turn ('right now') and the end of it ('we've got the instructions anyway'). In a way, another feature, which is almost exclusive to speaking and rare in writing, the **tag question** can also serve a similar purpose. The 'isn't it' and 'don't you' which litter informal conversation may act like regular questions and invite an answer. But they have many different functions, such as seeking confirmation (you spell it with -e, don't you?), drawing someone out (you've just got back from the States, haven't you?) or expressing various emotions, such as surprise, horror or disbelief (he didn't say that, did he?). Intonation is the major means of performing the desired function and without it, in a written transcript, we can't always be sure of the function or it may serve more than one purpose. Here with 'I've done it the wrong way round, have I?' the speaker seems to start off by intending to seek confirmation but if this were to be fully realised, we'd expect to find 'haven't I'. Maybe the speaker becomes unsure – maybe she's done it right after all – and moves to question herself.

Tag questions are quite complex and a fuller discussion can be found in *The Language of Conversation* (Pridham, 2001) and *Working with Texts* (Carter *et al.*, 2001) but for the purposes of the discussion here, tag questions very much reflect the interactive nature of conversation.

Activity

In Unit 2, we looked at the face-saving conversation of the teenagers on their way home from school. Here, the conversation has been tampered with so that it's no longer authentic. Which natural language features are absent? Which unrealistic language features have been incorporated? (You might like to turn to page 29 to compare.)

A: Would you ever ask a teacher to explain something?

B: No, I would never do that! Everyone would really HATE you, don't you think so?

A: Yes, I do. I would wait until afterwards for a private word. What about you, Chris?

C: Yes, I agree. You'd sound stupid and it would be so embarrassing!

Commentary

In normal conversations, even with adjacency pairs, we don't have to rely on a question/answer format – utterances can be offered uninvited. In the version in Unit 2, one statement overlaps with another. The participants pick up on the various clues we've mentioned – discourse markers, intonation, etc. – which indicate that it's acceptable to join in at a suitable moment. Contributions don't have to be equal in length, nor follow set patterns of length, as with long question/short answer, nor be evenly distributed amongst the participants. We don't always produce full grammatical sentences but use ellipsis and contractions.

Activity

Many of the features we've looked at overlap, so that tag questions, for example, are grammatical in construction, yet have discoursal functions. Of course, in any conversation, many of these language features occur simultaneously so we need to take a longer stretch of conversation and see all of these features in action.

Read Text: Cooking rice, which is part of a longer conversation recorded in the kitchen of a family home; all the participants are members of the same family. No external person was present to supervise the recording but they were all aware of the presence of the tape-recorder and make reference to it. Before looking at the commentary, make notes on any features which seem particularly characteristic of spoken language.

Text: Cooking rice

```
 1  <S 04>  what you making Ian?
 2  <S 02>  mm
 3  <S 04>  what's that?
 4  <S 02>  oh er just gonna do some rice
 5  <S 04>  mm
 6  <S 02>  doing some rice in the micro
 7  <S 03>  so you put margarine with it
 8  <S 02>  pardon yeah little bit don't know why cos otherwise it'll
 9  <S 03>  separate it
10  <S 02>  mm not sure actually doesn't erm don't have to do it when you put it
11          on the er on the stove
12  <S 03>  how long does it take?
13  <S 02>  erm
14  <S 01>  oh that'll make a noise
15  <S 02>  takes about thirty-five minutes yeah that'll that
16          that'll destroy your tape
17  <S 03>  thirty-five minutes
18  <S 02>  yeah
19  <S 01>  yeah
20  <S 03>  I thought the microwave did everything in about two minutes
21  <S 01>  you may as well turn it off now then
22  <S 03>  yeah you can do it on the cooker for this in thirty-five minutes
23  <S 02>  then if you have to watch it . . . you just ignore it
24  <S 03>  mm
25  <S 04>  you don't have to wash the saucepan either do you?
26  <S 02>  you don't have to wash the saucepan after [laughs] [<S 03> mm] you
27          don't have to erm don't have to drain the water off either
28  <S 03>  I didn't know that microwaves ran that long
29  <S 02>  yeah you don't have to erm drain the water off either cos er
30  <S 03>  I'll switch it off when you turn that on
31  <S 02>  when Sahib used to come out and make rice and your saucepan
32          used to be it'd be thick about an inch thick on the bottom it would
33          and that was the best part of the rice
```

Commentary

We've already given you the context of this interaction so that you know where it takes place, the setting, and the nature of the participants. If we hadn't told you, the cookery-related lexis would have given the first away and there are many aspects of the language and the discourse structure which indicate the familiar, intimate nature of the participants' relationship. They are all actively interested in the ongoing action, asking genuine questions, reinforcing each other's comments and sharing similar thoughts and jokes. The conversation is co-operative and smooth.

The first thing you'll have noticed is the messy nature of spoken language when transcribed in writing. Sometimes it's quite difficult to follow, with so many unfinished utterances and pronoun references ('it' here referring to the rice or the microwave).

Some of the features you should have noticed are as follows but the commentary is not exhaustive:

- ellipsis – 1, 4, 8
- deixis – 3
- hesitation – 2, 10
- vague language – 4 ('some'), 8 ('little bit')
- pronunciation features – 4 (attempt to represent connected speech with 'gonna'), 8 ('cos')
- false start – 4/6 ('gonna do' reformulated to 'doing')
- back-channel – 5
- grammatical statement functioning as request for confirmation – 7
- filler – 10 ('actually')
- repetition – 10
- discourse marker – 21
- question tag – 25
- incomplete clause – 23, 29
- co-ordination – 31–33 ('and')

These are all localised features but it's also important to look at language across the entire stretch of the extract: at how language is recycled or follows a track and is picked up by either the same speaker or another. Here you can trace various references throughout to the rice, the microwave and relative advantages of different cooking methods. We can see the co-operative and interpersonal nature of the exchanges as speakers reinforce each other, indicate agreement and like-mindedness. The speaking accompanies actions but, whereas in the Text: Doing a job much of the language was part of the activity, here the language has a far more social function and the activity is used as a social focal point for interaction rather than a vital element to get something done.

Activity

In Unit 5, we'll be comparing the language of speech and writing but before reading about it, you might like to look back and compare the written recipe texts from Unit 3, from a language perspective, with this dialogue here. Do the features highlighted here as characteristic of spoken language have any parallels in the written language?

Functions of speech

We've said all along that all communication is purpose-driven; we've also said that in spoken language there can be a mismatch between 'accurate' grammar and the utterance. These two are connected in that we produce spoken utterances which convey our purpose – to persuade, apologise, congratulate; they are functional first and foremost – and the grammar fits accordingly but not necessarily accurately, in purist terms.

In line 7 of the Text: Cooking rice, the speaker says 'so you put margarine with it'. Grammatically speaking, this is an incomplete sentence but on the page it reads more like a statement than a question. Functionally speaking, on the other hand, the speaker might be checking for confirmation and/or registering surprise.

If we take an example from an earlier unit, the phone call to the Greek tourist office in Unit 2, the problem of discontinuity we found there was not solely related to turntaking. Remember, the caller said: 'I wondered if you had any free tourist literature on Rhodes'. The function, as intended by the speaker, is a request for action. We could translate it bluntly as 'Please send me some free tourist literature'. It isn't even a direct question although it elicits the response 'Yes' as if it were. It's a statement, declaring a personal thought ('I wondered'). Because of the lack of uptake, the speaker has to reformulate: 'could you send me some please'.

The first utterance is indirect and therefore runs the risk of not being understood or being misinterpreted. Sometimes we need to be direct and explicit in order to achieve our purposes effectively but there's a compromise to be struck in order to be effective without giving offence unintentionally (see considerations of face in Unit 5).

Directness and indirectness relate very closely to the face-to-face nature of spoken interaction and are not commonly associated with writing. However, once again it's unwise to be categorical – the two letters in Unit 3 showed it was relevant in those instances, just as it is in other written contexts, such as academic assignments, for example.

Activity

These are all authentic utterances heard in conversation. They are all indirect. What do you think they mean? What function are they intended to perform? How would you convert them to be more direct? What effect would this have?

1   Hotel resident to breakfast restaurant waiter:
    I'll just have some toast if I could.

2   Shop assistant comes out of the shop to speak to a window shopper:
    If you need anything, I'm inside the shop.

3   College student in shared hall of residence kitchen:
    Is this anyone's margarine?

4   Restaurant customer to waiter (TV's *Mr Bean* sketch):
    Are these oysters all right?

5   Person waiting in queue to someone not waiting in queue:
    There's a queue.

6   Railway guard to skate-boarding youngster on platform:
    This isn't a skating rink!

Conclusion

The real-time nature of spontaneous conversation is a highly influential factor, producing numerous instances of the following:

◎   pauses;
◎   hesitation;
◎   false starts;
◎   fillers.

The effects of this on the grammar of conversation can be summarised as:

- simple clauses;
- contractions;
- ellipsis;
- straightforward word order (unless for specific reasons).

The lexis of everyday speech tends to be:

- simple;
- general;
- verb-based more than noun-based;
- vague.

It may have evidence of original creativity.

Discourse features relate to the interactive nature of conversational speech and include the following:

- adjacency pairs;
- back-channelling;
- discourse markers;
- question tags.

The functional nature of spoken language leads to grammatical forms which may belie the purpose and can involve indirectness.

However messy spoken interaction appears to be from analysing written transcriptions, with unfinished utterances and false starts, it shouldn't be forgotten that, for the most part, people are highly efficient at communicating exactly what they want to.

While the face-to-face, interactive nature of conversation of course affects the language, it's the pressure of time which is highly influential on many language features and forms such a contrast with written language.

Extension

1   With permission, tape-record an informal discussion between friends or relatives. Transcribe one section and see what proportion is made up of general words and vague language.

2   Look again at the Text: Doing a job, the cot-assembling dialogue. Choose a short section and re-write it to make it sound as unrealistic as you can. Write a detailed comparative commentary of the changes made.

3   Devise a worksheet in which you describe some common conversational situations. For example: You sit down in a café and find

no menu on the table. What do you say to the waiter? Try to think of about ten different situations in which you vary the nature of the participants and the context. Make sure you describe each situation in enough detail for your worksheet respondents to be able to understand fully.

Either (a) ask as many people, from a variety of backgrounds, as possible to fill in the worksheet on paper or (b) set up tape-recorded interviews. If possible, try to compare your responses with naturally-occurring examples in real conversations.

The relationship between speech and writing

Aims of this unit

The aims of this unit are to draw together strands from the two preceding units in order to study the factors which affect the choice between communicating in speech or in writing and to analyse the effects of these factors on the language used in each case.

Choosing whether to speak or to write

In *The Cambridge Encyclopedia of Language*, Crystal states that if we're in the same room as someone we wish to communicate with 'We do not write to each other when we have the opportunity to speak – apart from such exceptional cases as secretive children in class and spouses who are "not talking"' (Crystal, 1991, p. 178) but maybe that's over-simplifying the case. So, what are the rules of societal conduct which dictate whether we speak or write?

Activity

Consider the following situations and decide whether you would choose to conduct them in writing or speech:

1   Making a booking for
     (a)   a train ticket
     (b)   a holiday
     (c)   a hall for a party
     (d)   student accommodation

2   Expressing emotions such as
     (a)   love
     (b)   sympathy on a bereavement
     (c)   congratulations on exam results
     (d)   commiseration on exam results

3   Applying for
     (a)   a vacation job
     (b)   a college course
     (c)   a university prospectus
     (d)   a voluntary position on a committee

4   Giving instructions on
     (a)   how to work a piece of equipment
     (b)   how to cook a certain dish
     (c)   how to get somewhere
     (d)   how to perform a lifesaving action

5   Conducting studies
     (a)   for internal coursework
     (b)   for internal assessment
     (c)   for external examinations

Commentary

You may have found it difficult to decide absolutely on one form or another without knowing a little more about the precise nature of the communication event or you may have decided on a combined approach, such as for 3, speaking on the phone first and following up with a letter. Nevertheless, some factors of the situation will have influenced your choice and in turn the style and language used. We look at the former now and turn to the latter afterwards.

Factors affecting choice

Beneath each of the factors is a response (R), taken from a student questionnaire, which typifies the students' feelings in each respect and may resemble your own feelings.

◎   **face-to-face** – it may or may not be desirable to be face to face with the receiver in order to get immediate feedback which would allow for negotiation.

R: The word 'confrontation' appeared again and again. Non-face-to-face exchanges are far less confrontational. One student, however, preferred speaking to writing because with the latter 'you don't know what the response is going to be'.

◎ **face** – we may find a situation potentially embarrassing or awkward or we may think that it might be so for the receiver.

R: Frequent mention was made of embarrassing talks with parents regarding 'the BIG talk, serious stuff such as sex, contraception, drugs'.

R: 'If the subject is good, then it is easier to speak out but if the situation is about death, for example, then you would prefer to write it down.' This was often termed, the 'easy way out'.

R: 'The person you're talking to might be disappointed or a bit angry and be a bit weird.'

◎ **permanency** – it may or may not be important to have a permanent record of a transaction for future reference and/or proof.

R: 'whether the information needs to be long-lasting or not'; 'to refer back to'.

◎ **clarity** – some situations demand absolute clarity; confusion can lead to dire consequences. With speech, particularly at a distance, such as over the phone, there is always the chance of being mis-heard whereas the permanency of the written word allows for clear confirmation at any time.

R: 'also the length of an instruction and how complicated the matter is'.

◎ **competence** – either perceived or in reality, we may feel more skilled in one medium than in another for a particular situation.

R: 'I don't know what to say to people who are upset.'

R: 'I find it easier to write down instructions than telling someone how to do something.'

[I would prefer not to write essays because] 'I often find them difficult.'

[I would rather not write job application forms because] 'I find it difficult to talk about myself.'

- **speed/urgency** – the real-time nature of spoken discourse is a highly influential factor, particularly in the case of life and death, but in normal situations too, speed may be a deciding factor.

  R: 'speech is quicker'; 'writing is slower'.

- **formality** – there is a perception that the more formal expressions are more suitable to writing whereas speaking is better for more informal and more personal exchanges.

  R: [writing is more suitable for] 'a more formal situation such as a job application'; 'formal memorable situations need writing'.

- **planning** – some situations and some language events need more planning than others which will work perfectly well spontaneously.

  R: [writing preferred to speaking for such topics as] 'Politics or religion – would prefer to consider the issues and gather information.'

  R: [writing for giving instructions preferred in order to] 'plan directions'.

- **personal issues** – to express emotions, one medium may be more suitable than another. The closeness of the relationship will also affect choice.

  R: 'sometimes it means more to speak your feelings' but many talked of avoiding speaking about personal problems altogether.

  R: 'Sometimes it would depend on how close you were to someone.'

  R: [condolence on] 'bereavement is better spoken as someone's voice can sometimes be comforting'.

- **social conventions** – norms of interaction may exist which make one medium the more obvious choice.

  R: Most students felt it was more usual to write in order to apply for a job or a prospectus and to book rooms.

  R: From another group of students comes a reminder that people can have different ideas about these conventions, depending on culture, gender or age.

R: A young mother thought it usual to ring up a college to enquire verbally about a course but when she advised her son to do this, he said he thought an email would be far better in getting to the target person more directly and more immediately.

You will probably have realised that there is some overlap in some of these factors and many work in combination, rather than singly, to affect our choices.

Activity

For each of the factors listed above, think of a situation in which a) the feature is a major consideration, and b) in which it would be ridiculous or harmful to operate in another medium.

Commentary

You should have found many situations to discuss. Here is just one authentic written text as an example.

ORDERING REPEAT PRESCRIPTIONS

From 1st April 2000 it will no longer be possible to order repeat prescriptions over the telephone. ALL requests must be made in writing, preferably using the GREEN re-order slip.

MANY drug names sound very similar and we are concerned that a serious mistake may be made when drug names are (MIS)read over the telephone.

In a situation such as this, dire consequences can result from lack of clarity of speech heard at a distance (over the phone). By forcing the written alternative, you introduce the permanency factor, to allow for proof of record.

Effects on language

What kind of effects might these factors have on linguistic features? We've taken here a few from the list. (All the examples are authentic.)

Face to face

Spoken

A: so you put margarine with it
B: pardon yeah little bit don't know why cos otherwise it'll
A: separate it

The face-to-face nature of everyday conversation makes it easy for the exchange participants to co-operate and negotiate meaning as they go along. If a speaker isn't sure of the facts, or is having trouble searching for a word, the participant can see that immediately and, depending on the relationship, help out, provide information, or, as here, supply a word, and allow the conversation to continue. Conversation, then, is not just one utterance separated from another but very much a joint venture, relying on audible and visible clues – facial gestures, body language, intonation, hesitancy features, etc. – to enable speakers to judge what is required at the time and make adjustments as necessary. It also accounts for some seeming ungrammaticality in speech as, in isolation, B's utterance is incomplete (a 'non-finite sentence', in grammatical terms) but taking the exchange as a whole, we find it is in fact complete because of A's final contribution.

Written

Notice in hotel bedroom: 'Smoke alarms are fitted in every room and are highly sensitive.'

In other words, don't smoke in here! It would, of course, be totally unrealistic to expect hotel managers to speak to each guest individually about house rules, so standard instructions of one kind or another are produced in the written medium to save time, ensure consistency and provide permanent proof.

Although styles vary, and this is quite an extreme example in its hint-like quality, such written instructions are designed for the general, unknown reader and must therefore be clear and inoffensive. This is realised by using an impersonal style and avoiding the mention of a human agent, such as the hotel manager, and referring instead to 'Smoke alarms'. A passive verb ('are fitted') is therefore used and the text remains descriptive, leaving it up to the reader to make the necessary inference.

Face

Spoken

Train guard to passenger: 'There's no smoking in these compartments.' The guard, even though he has the authority to give a direct order, presumably finds the situation confrontational. To lessen the dictatorial tone, and to remove the responsibility from himself, he uses an impersonal style by stating the rule ('There's no smoking').

Written

Printed notice in English supermarket restaurant: 'We respectfully request that only food purchased in the restaurant is consumed on the premises. Thank you.'

Once again, the store manager would be within rights to forbid directly. Instead, in a style often parodied as 'typically British' in its politeness, the inclusive pronoun 'we' is less threatening, the formal lexis ('request', 'purchased', 'consumed', 'premises') conveys an official, but not officious, tone, and the passive voice is less confrontational than the active ('you consume'). The final closure of thanks, in imitation of a spoken exchange, rounds things off nicely.

Urgency

Spoken

'Get out, quick!'

It's obvious that, in life and death situations, speech is the most appropriate in its immediacy. For extreme urgency, language has to be cut down to the bare minimum – here, the imperative verb ('get out') is the briefest form, without the need for pronouns or lengthy clauses.

Written

'This bomb is set to explode in 30 minutes.'

The urgency will naturally be conveyed by the situation. However, the language is clear and unambiguous so that it can be interpreted quickly. Again, the impersonal style with the passive ('is set') is suitable in its clarity and in its avoidance of naming the responsible party.

Social conventions

Spoken

'I do.'

    According to social conventions, people getting married have to declare certain vows orally which are then legally enforced in writing. Certain stock phrases become part of such official ceremonies and are rarely heard out of context ('I name this ship', 'I sentence you'). In some cases, only certain people with the right qualifications and/or status have the 'power' to say such phrases and bring about the associated outcome.

Written

'Dear Sir . . . Yours faithfully'

    Social conventions dictate that certain things should be carried out in writing but these may not be the same in every culture and they may change over a period of time either as social requirements or preferences change or as new technology develops. At one time, it was normal in Britain to inform domestic services in writing of a change of occupancy, etc. but today, letters often get left on someone's desk whereas a phone call gets an immediate response.

    British English formal letter writing has established conventions of phraseology particularly related to greetings. Although punctuation rules have become relaxed, it's still traditional to match the beginning and ending of a formal letter as above (just as 'Dear + name' and 'Yours sincerely' go together).

Activity

Using either the same categories, or others from the earlier list, think of some contrastive examples of written and spoken language. Analyse the differences of grammar, lexis and style.

A question of degree

We've established that spoken discourse and written discourse are not one and the same thing. It's tempting to think of them as polar opposites and make definitive statements such as 'Speech is informal' and 'Writing is permanent'. Many students in our survey made similar claims, typically: 'In formal cases writing is more appropriate than speaking which is more suited to informal situations.'

You might find some such statements earlier in this book. That's fine to start with but things rarely come so neatly packaged. There are some qualities which are shared by both media and so, rather than talking in absolute terms, we need to think more of degree and relativity. Another of the students in the survey wrote 'Speech – more personal, transient; writing – more formal, permanent.' It's the comparative *more* which is so important.

Think of an imaginary line with two extremes at either end; there's a whole range of positions at various points *along* the line. Different texts will have features in varying degrees and can therefore be positioned at different points on such a **cline** or continuum. Then the texts, and the features, can be compared and contrasted.

Features of spoken and written texts

Here we look more closely at some specific points of comparison and contrast. Below are some aspects to consider with some contrastive genres, both written (W) and spoken (S), as examples.

Permanent?

Myth: *All writing is permanent. All speech is temporary.*

Permanency of speech is hard to achieve: we usually need to employ artificial means, such as audio-recorders or written transcriptions, to record speech for the future.

Formal?

Myth: *All writing is formal. All speech is informal.*

There is a link, as you can see, between the formality of permanent discourse and the informality of more transient discourse.

Interactive?

Myth: *Writing is one-way. Speech is interactive.*

less interactive   more interactive

W: poster   text messages

S: lecture   chat

Informative?

Myth: *Writing conveys important information. Speaking is personal and social.*

message-oriented   socially-oriented

W: recipe   greetings card

S: weather forecast   greetings on meeting

Context-dependent?

Myth: *All texts depend on context to the same degree.*

Perhaps some clarification is needed with this: all discourse depends on context but some texts can *only* be understood with reference to something external to the text (or to another text) while other texts are self-contained and create their own internal context.

low dependency   high dependency

W: fictional work   equipment instruction leaflet

S: poetry recital   oral directions

There is obviously some overlap here; some of the genres could be used to exemplify other features and this list of features is by no means exhaustive. Keep this in mind during the next activity.

Copy the clines above into your notebook. (Remember they are clines which means that you do not need to keep to polar opposites but can consider a greater or lesser degree of each aspect.) Plot the following types of discourse on to suitable positions on the relevant cline. The same discourse type can be used for more than one cline. Then try to add some more of your own.

Spoken	Written
conversation about weather	personal diary entry
news broadcast	newspaper article
job interview	blackmail note
gossip	stock-taking report
presidential address	office memo
telephone banking	profile to accompany CV
hijacker's threat	message in time capsule
teacher input	car maintenance manual
answer-machine message	horoscope

Text and language

So far, this has looked at qualities of texts and representative genres but, as always, we need to focus on language and see how this relates to the discussion. One example from the clines given above can be used as a starting-point.

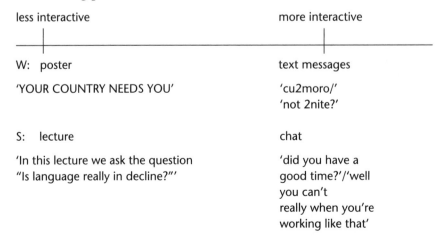

less interactive   more interactive

W: poster   text messages

'YOUR COUNTRY NEEDS YOU'   'cu2moro/'
                                                  'not 2nite?'

S: lecture   chat

'In this lecture we ask the question   'did you have a
"Is language really in decline?"'   good time?'/'well
                                                  you can't
                                                  really when you're
                                                  working like that'

There are many points to note here. For example, a poster isn't necessarily written in an impersonal, formal style. It can 'speak' directly to the reader (see Unit 6) but, like the lecture example, it doesn't expect a verbal response. The lecture question is rhetorical, introducing the lecture answer. Grammatically, then, statements *and* questions can be non-interactive. Likewise, a written text doesn't have to be longer and more carefully constructed than its oral counterpart. It, as can be seen here, can employ abbreviations and formulae (also discussed further in Unit 6) to make it even shorter and more casual than oral interaction. However, the text message and verbal chat are based on true exchanges, questions or prompts which expect, and get, a response.

From this, it can be seen that the polar positions on the clines given above are simplifications and that the examples could be placed on different positions and more extreme text types found for both ends. It also shows that each text type is an idealisation and that, without the language, we can't know anything for certain.

Text comparison

To see the comparison of language in action, we need to compare a spoken text with a written text. Because of the different nature of the two media, it isn't always easy to find similar texts to compare. The following pair of texts has advantages and disadvantages: as this was set up as an experiment, it's not totally authentic. However, the control of the experiment allows for two texts on the same theme to be compared and contrasted.

The Text: Interview with Louise was conducted without a script on either part. The interviewer simply told the interviewee, Louise, beforehand that she was going to be asked some questions about accent. Louise is the interviewer's niece so the setting and tone is quite informal. Louise was then asked to produce a written text on the topic which she did about a month later (Text: Written version of interview). This meant that the theme hadn't been totally forgotten but the actual language used in the interview could not be replicated from memory.

Activity

Read through the Text: Interview with Louise and make notes about any language features which seem characteristic of spoken language (refer to Unit 4 and the preceding section of this unit). You might also consider what

84

features are characteristic of an interview, as opposed to a totally uncontrolled conversation. Can you identify any language which reflects the participants' relationship?

Text: Interview with Louise

I = Interviewer   L = Louise

I: right Louise when did you (.) first go to university

L: er late September (.) 99

I: right and (.) you're living (.) with (.) a lot people from different areas

L: yeah that's right

I: how many and where do they come from

L: um there's 19 (.) people including me there's (1) one girl from London

I: mm

L: 2 people from up north in Leeds (.) there's um a couple of South Africans, (1) Germans, French um what else (1) Americans

I: any more from from Britain

L: er (1) some people (.) lived abroad and then moved back to Britain so there's probably about 4

I: right and

L: altogether

I: did *you* notice anything about your accent changing or did *they* notice anything about *your* accent when you . . . did you . . . did it come up at all

L: they teased me for being an Essex [inaudible – laughter] Essex accent

I: yeah

L: certain things I say but .

I: wha what sort of things (1) can you remember what they teased you about

L: um the way (.) I end things

I: right

L: I can't think of any other word but other than the word flabby they would like *flabbay* [laughter] sort of thing

I: so they they mimicked you and

L: yeah

I: and you laughed about it

L: yeah

I: right

L: I joked about their accents as well

[fault on tape obliterates the question which was to do with whether this affected the way Louise spoke]

L: I suppose (.) pronounce things more clearly

I: mm

L: because, especially the Americans, they didn't understand [barely audible – what you were] saying and the Germans as well so you had to

I: right

L: pronounce things so slight difference

I: yeah

L: that way I suppose

I: and and when when they teased you, did you make any conscious effort to change how you spoke

L: no

I: no so you think

L: no it was it was only friendly

I: yeah yeah

I: so you think you speak the same as you did before you left

L: no [laughs]

I: what how do you think it's changed

L: um it's more(.) I don't know more properly spoken I suppose (1) clearer

I: and you've done that because they didn't understand you particularly

L: yeah and (1)yeah I suppose so
. . .

I: and were you aware when you came home from being in London that um Mum or anybody else noticed that you spoke differently

L: yeah

I: what what did they say to you

L: they said you've got your North London voice on
. . .

I: but you weren't aware of any difference or did you notice yourself

L: I noticed that I started going back into more sort of um (3) . . . what's the word I don't know but like you go in this ouse you know sort of thing a bit more Essexy I suppose

Activity

Now read the written-up account of the interview and highlight any features which represent points of comparison and contrast with the spoken text. This is the version Louise produced as a written text. No instructions were given as to text type, readership, etc., only as to the theme (as that of the interview).

Text: Written version of interview

I lived in Essex for most of my life, until I moved to London approximately 8 months ago, in order to attend university. Since then I (and other people) have noticed a change in the way I talk. My house in London is home to 19 people, who come from all over the world (e.g. USA, South Africa, Germany, Israel, Botswana, etc.) and have varying accents. At first I, like the others, was teased about my accent and pronunciation (in a friendly way). For instance, pronouncing house as owse and happy as happieeee! After a while though, the differences in speech seemed to be unimportant, and the teasing for all members of the house fizzled out. When I returned to Essex the teasing recommenced. I was told by my family that my manner of speaking resembled a posh North London schoolgirl! This I disagree with, thinking instead that it is actually a combination of the accents from the people with whom I live (i.e. a 'worldwide' accent).

Commentary

The first thing to mention is the length of the transcript of the spoken interview: pages of print for a conversation which took just two minutes! Not to mention the length of time it took to transcribe the recording. In the written text, the same amount of information is communicated but in much less reading time and physical space.

A second point is that the act of writing down a spoken event alters it and makes it seem very unnatural. It's often quite boring, sometimes difficult, to read transcripts of conversations; the written text is easy and straightforward to read and understand.

Very often, little of what is actually said in casual conversation could be called 'concrete' and so the text is made up of a large proportion of fillers and repetition. The nature of this interview, however, focusing on a central thematic topic, means that quite a lot of information is actually conveyed and transferred.

The written text displays many more features of formal language than the spoken text. The spoken text reveals several clues as to the relationship of the speakers – relaxed informal style with frequent laughter; the interviewer's familiarity with certain facts so that instead of a direct question, a statement is used with intonation functioning as a request for confirmation ('you're living with a lot of people'); the use of 'Mum' as opposed to 'your mother' and so on.

- Typical features – All the typical, non-fluency features of spoken English discussed in Units 2 and 4 occur here: ellipsis, false starts, repetition, pausing, hesitation and fillers ('you know', 'sort of thing', 'er', 'um', 'pronounce things'). The written text has all the typical features of sentence formation, spelling, punctuation and so on.
- Sentence construction – The written text has longer sentences with complex structures involving relative clauses ('19 people, who come from all over the world', 'the people with whom I live'). In the interview, shorter sentences are used with the repeated structure of the introductory 'There' ('There's 19 people', 'there's one girl', 'there's um a couple of').
- Word order – The spoken text has normal word order. In the written text, position of clauses has been carefully controlled, particularly placing linked clauses close together ('I and other people', 'the teasing for all members'). Most noticeable is the 'unusual' positioning of the object before the subject ('This I disagree with') which doesn't commonly feature in everyday spoken language.
- Verbs – Most of the verbs in the interview are in the active voice ('they teased me', 'they said you've got'). In the written text, the passive occurs ('I . . . was teased', 'I was told').
- Deixis – In the spoken text, 'from up north' is in direct relation to the current location of being in London ('down south'). The written text makes no such connection.
- Time relationships – Various differences can be found. In the interview, the date is given more precisely than in the written text which might seem unusual – possibly Louise was ready for this first question ('late September 99' v. 'approximately 8 months ago'). This second example, from the written text, is deictic in that its meaning is only clear in relation to the present time. In the written text, the time relationship between events is stated explicitly ('Since then', 'After a while'). In the interview, time either isn't mentioned or it's implicit from the interviewer's question.
- Formality – Far more monosyllabic words and simple words, often of

Anglo-Saxon origin, feature in the interview responses ('lived', 'joked', 'started'). In the written text, longer words are used and words of other language origins, noticeably here French ('resembled', 'recommended', 'home to').

◎ Creativity – We have, in the spoken text, an example of individual creativity with the word 'Essexy', as discussed in Unit 4. This time a noun, in fact a place name (and they tend to be fairly fixed in English), has been converted into an adjective by the addition of the common suffix -y, meaning 'having the quality of', as in *creamy*. The motivation for this is uncertain. Humour? Vagueness? But by comparison, no creative words appear in the written version.

◎ Representation – It's extremely difficult to represent pronunciation in writing without resorting to a phonetic alphabet. Of course, in the original interview, the voice successfully conveys the intended sounds ('flabbay', 'ouse') so in the written text, a writer has to use spelling, and maybe punctuation, to represent the spoken sounds ('owse', 'happieeee!').

◎ Contractions – In the spoken text, contractions are common ('there's', 'can't', 'don't') but the full forms are used in writing ('I have noticed', 'it is').

◎ **Prosody** – Once again, it's difficult to represent in written form all the associated features of spoken language, related to intonation, pitch, stress and pace and this hasn't been attempted here. However, they can reflect meaning and attitude. The pitch of the voice dropped considerably on 'didn't understand *what you were* saying' and on 'what's the word'. The voice tends to drop on unimportant asides, some grammar words or if we feel uncertain or need time to think. Pace was noticeable in the rapid response to the question 'did you make any conscious effort to change how you spoke?' The immediate reply 'no' conveyed strength of commitment, possibly also humour.

◎ Function – The oral interview is, by its nature, a discussion, with the questions prompting facts and inviting the interviewee to reflect on a given topic. The purpose of opening prompts is to set the context and provide the background which is needed in order to make sense of later contributions. The responses answer questions or develop points further; they relate past events and gives reasons. The written text narrates past events, giving examples. It states an opinion and a justification.

Conclusion

For the most part, choices between writing and speaking go on all the time without conscious decision-making. It might be determined by factors largely out of our control. On other occasions, we make a particular choice, taking the relevant factors into consideration.

We *can* convey similar messages either in speaking or writing because our purpose may be the same (to offer condolences, to make a reservation, etc.) but the language will vary between the two. We rarely write and speak in identical language and features of particular difference relate to:

◎   grammar;
◎   vocabulary;
◎   style.

In all cases, however, texts reflect these differences in varying degrees. It's important to keep in mind that speaking and writing are not absolute opposites of each other, one should not be defined in terms of the other and that everything is a matter of degree rather than absolutes.

Extension

Making a selection from the text types you've plotted on the clines, give an example of written and spoken language for each one. Compare the language with that of texts on different positions on the same cline. Consider if you now need to alter your original plotted positions.

Where boundaries meet

Aims of this unit

The aim of this unit is to analyse texts, both written and spoken, which display features usually associated with the other medium.

The purpose of the text

When studying language in use and analysing texts, it's very easy, and in some ways necessary, to look at clear-cut examples and reach firm conclusions. Everything gets parcelled up into neat and tidy bundles. A basic human desire is to solve riddles, to clear up mysteries – to put the final piece in the jigsaw. Unfortunately, no actual human endeavour is that simple. For every solution you come up with, half a dozen more questions come to light. The same is true with the study of speech and writing.

We've looked at the nature and analysed the language of each. We've even plotted texts on a continuum according to the degree to which they exhibit individual features. Even so, you could probably go out right now and find hundreds of texts which don't seem to 'fit the rules'; they don't match up in every respect; they don't play the game. Maybe you've already done that as you've gone along. If so, that's great. It means you've realised that you can't take anything for granted with language and that you've become aware of language in action around you.

We can't dismiss them as simple 'exceptions' – because of course there are no hard and fast rules of which they could *be* exceptions. Instead we have to analyse them closely and see exactly what's going on and see if we can come up with some new conclusions.

We've said all along that language is purpose-driven and this is absolutely fundamental. The question you need to ask is *what was the purpose of producing this text?* Once we know the purpose, it's easier then to look at the means by which the purpose has been achieved. But we don't live in a perfect world. Millions of texts are being constantly produced and so it stands to reason that not all of them will be brilliant; not all of them will achieve their purpose; some of them could have been more effective if handled differently. There is also the possibility that the purpose of the text producer doesn't match with that of the text receiver. For example, a company produces an advert to try to sell its product; the reader may simply read for amusement or for language study. However, if the text is authentic rather than adapted for some different purpose, the producer's purpose is a major concern as that will have determined the context and language. You will need, therefore, to bear in mind the original purpose of each text as you come to analyse it in this unit.

Written texts which use features of spoken texts

We said in Unit 5 that writing and speaking are not at opposite ends of the spectrum. In fact, the spectrum image is a useful one. In the spectrum, you can clearly identify a colour, yellow, for example, and you can identify its neighbour, orange. There's a fuzzy area where the two overlap where it's impossible to say where the yellow has finished and the orange begun. Sometimes, text boundaries blur in the same kind of way. We might read a text, so it's obviously a written text, but it might have features we would normally associate with spoken texts – and vice versa.

Advertising companies realise how effective and dynamic spoken language is. The highly successful British Gas 'Creature Comforts' campaign exploited this to the full by actually putting spontaneous, naturally occurring dialogue into the mouths of animated creatures.

Activity

Many companies still produce printed adverts and try to avoid any written features which might distance, or alienate, the reader/potential customer, such as those related to an impersonal or formal style. The way to do this is to adopt a spoken 'voice' – to seem to speak to us and so draw us into their world. We hear, in our heads, a voice speaking directly to us; it's highly personal and very effective. Look at the Text: Daewoo cars and consider the features used.

Text: Daewoo cars

4). 6 year anti-corrosion warranty. 5). 30 day /1,000 mile money back or exchange guarantee. 6). Free courtesy car. 7). Pick up and return of your car for service if needed. Mainland UK only. 8). Fixed purchase price with no hidden extras. 9). Delivery included. 10). Number plates included. 11). 12 months road tax included. 12). Full tank of fuel. 13). Metallic paint included. 14). Electronic ABS. 15). Driver's airbag. 16). Side impact protection. 17). Power steering. 18). Engine immobiliser. 19). Security glass etching. 20). Mobile phone. 21). Free customer helpline. For more information, call us on 0800 666 222.

A car company that doesn't use dealers? That'll be the Daewoo.

BY SELLING DIRECT THROUGH OUR OWN SHOWROOMS, IT'S NOT JUST THE DEALER'S COMMISSION WE CUT OUT.

Daewoo sell direct. This doesn't mean we sell our cars over the phone. It means we don't use dealers. By cutting out the middlemen (you'll like this bit), we pass the savings on to you. That way we give you more with your car as standard, and can ensure the level of service you get when you visit one of our showrooms. All prices are fixed. There are no hidden extras. Delivery is free. As are number plates, 12 months road tax and a full tank of petrol. In other words, the price you see on our car is the price you pay to put it on the road. Those prices range from £8,445 to £12,895 for the 3, 4 and 5 door Nexia and the Espero Saloon. That's not all. Here's what else you get as standard. 1). 3 year/60,000 mile free servicing including parts and labour. 2). 3 year/60,000 mile comprehensive warranty. 3). 3 year Daewoo Total AA Cover.

DAEWOO

Commentary

This ad for Daewoo cars appeared in the press as one of a series in a campaign. The main aspect which the company is trying to promote, as being quite revolutionary and different from its competitors, is its direct sales approach. This, it is hoped, will be a major attraction and once this has been impressed on the consumer, further details can be added. But this is not a straightforward, written paragraph, impersonally describing the attributes of the company and its cars – probably few people would read that, unless they were avid fans probably reading specialist literature. In the popular press, a different style has been adopted.

Remember our earlier discussion about graphics, images and so on? The image is very much a part of this text. It's a visual pun and one of great impact. The image is so well designed and well produced that we immediately interpret the association with language. The well-known, idiomatic phrase *to cut out the middleman* has been represented literally and visually.

Many jokes play with the contrast between idiomatic and literal meaning:

Q: What did E.T.'s mum say to him when he got home?
A: Where on earth have you been?

but not all phrases lend themselves to visuals. When found in the context of a real newspaper, the initial impact is even greater, as you have to look twice to see if the paper really has been torn out (to reveal the newsprint behind).

The language contains many features normally associated with spoken language: use of personal pronouns ('we', 'you'), short simple segments, contractions and, most noticeably, the jokey aside 'you'll like this bit', with the written parenthesis acting in place of intonation. The first statement, 'Daewoo sell direct', leads on to the second, 'This doesn't mean', which adjusts and clarifies the earlier one, much as we do in normal speech. Vocabulary is simple and informal ('this bit', 'cut out') and the final question is elliptied. This final line also imitates a two-turn dialogue, the question allowing the inclusion of Daewoo's slogan, in itself catchy in its colloquialism.

The first part impresses us with the savings to be made by not using dealers and then the numbered list piles on the effect of the large number of offers included in the package.

What is the purpose?

Many advertisements, not only for products but for jobs, particularly for non-executive posts appearing in the popular or local press, often adopt a similarly informal spoken style. The purpose behind this seems a combination of the following factors:

◎ by setting up a dialogue with the reader, the company adopts a 'voice' and therefore sounds human rather than distant and impersonal;

◎ by directly addressing the potential customer or applicant, the reader is drawn into the advertiser's world in a very personal way. He or she becomes directly involved which makes resistance that much harder;

◎ the language singles us out as individuals rather than one of the crowd and addresses us, not only on a one-to-one basis, but as an equal. There is no sense of intimidation or exclusion from the media or employment world.

It's thus a very powerful tool. In contrast, it's interesting to notice where it *isn't* employed. As we've said, ads for high-powered executives tend to adopt a more traditional, written style. Similarly, ads for 'serious' products, such as insurance policies, funeral services, etc., tend not to use spoken styles. This would seem to indicate that, at least in the perception of advertising agencies, spoken language might be thought to trivialise an issue, or be suitable for more lightweight matter, whereas written style can take a more neutral base.

Activity

Do some research in your local area – look out for ads which do, or do not, 'speak' to the customer. Look out for shop names which address the customer (Curl up and dye – hairdressers; Frying tonight – fish and chip shop) and compare them with similar shops that have gone for a more neutral tone (Hair design).

Also look at commercial brand names. Currently in Britain, margarine and mobile phone companies 'talk to us' ('I can't believe it's not butter', Pay as you Talk, Just Talk, etc.). Try some statistical analysis to find out the trends in your area. It might be possible to produce bar charts and then try to account for the trends.

Written texts which 'masquerade' as other text types

Take the ancient joke, When is a door not a door? When it's a jar (ajar). When is a newspaper article not a newspaper article? A dictionary definition not a dictionary definition? A novel not a novel? Once a genre is established and people recognise the format, that format can be 'borrowed' for another purpose.

Take another joke, for the moment, which illustrates this concept: An Englishman, an Irishman and a Scotsman walk into a pub and the landlord looks up at them and says, 'This is some kind of joke, isn't it?' The basis of this joke, the reason that it works, is because of the well-established format of the type of joke that traditionally begins, 'An Englishman, an Irishman and a Scotsman . . .'. We then have certain expectations of how the joke will proceed but most jokes, by their very nature, turn our expectations on their heels and give us a surprise ending. But we wouldn't be surprised, or amused, if we didn't know what to expect in the first place.

The same is true with a certain kind of written text which isn't all that it seems. There could be different reasons for such 'masquerading' texts. It might be to do with humour. It can simply be eye-catching, attention-getting. It might, because it assumes shared knowledge with the reader, have the effect of drawing the reader in closer to the writer, either to create a cosier, more intimate relationship, to make him/her feel part of an insider community, or part of the shared joke.

Intertextuality

We mentioned, in Unit 5, that some texts are comprehensible through reference to another kind of text but we didn't at that point introduce the term for this. **Intertextuality** is where one text relies on another for its interpretation to be successful. This feature tends to be associated with non-literary texts. The more literary a text is, the less it needs to rely on any other text for its interpretation and/or its impact. A literary text is self-contained and creates its own world of internal reference. All the following texts deliberately make use of features of another text type to create their desired effect.

Activity

As you look at each of the following written texts, consider before reading the commentary: What does it remind you of? What are the reasons for and the effects of producing texts in this way?

Text: Gadget

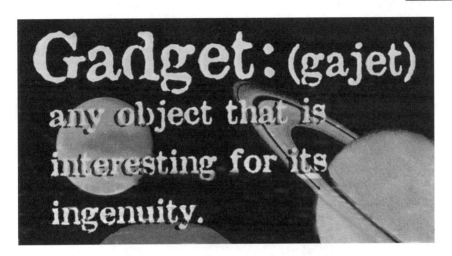

Gadget: (gajet)
any object that is
interesting for its
ingenuity.

Commentary

If you shop in The Gadget Shop, you could have found this definition on the plastic bag they give you, so you're not going to think for one minute that you have a page from a dictionary in your hands. However, it looks very like a dictionary definition, with the headword in larger print, phonetic transcript and the notational, ellipted style of many dictionaries – '[a gadget is] any object' – produced in a column layout. Probably most people go no further – if they go that far. It looks genuine and the definition sort of fits, so it could well be the genuine thing. However, if we compare it with the definition in the *New Shorter Oxford English Dictionary* online, we find:

gadget / 'gadZlt' / *n.*

119. [Origin unkn.]

1. Orig. Naut. A small device, mechanism, or fitting in a piece of machinery etc.; local (a vessel equipped with) a winch or small crane. 119.

2. gen. An accessory, an adjunct; a knick-knack, a gewgaw. e20.

There are many interesting differences – the greater phonetic detail, word class, origin dates – but in particular, one small grammatical difference is fundamental. The indefinite article ('a', 'an'), universally employed in standard English dictionaries, has been altered on the bag to the all-embracing 'any'. The adjectival phrase 'interesting for its ingenuity' is highly evaluative and of course reinforces the company's sales message whereas the dictionary simply lists alternative nouns with no description.

Text: HABURI.COM

HABURI.COM is threatening to destroy our livelihood. They are selling designer clothes for 25-70% less than the prices in our shops. It's outrageous! How can we compete and survive? And now, if that wasn't bad enough, they are offering an additional 20% discount, if you log on to their obnoxious web site www.haburi.com/discount. This cannot be allowed. We appeal to your conscience and ask you to help us in our struggle. Our entire existence will be threatened if you buy your clothes at HABURI.COM. We urge you to boycott

Offer ends on 09.06.00   Please do not throw this on the street

HABURI.COM

Commentary

The directive to 'BOYCOTT HABURI.COM' is pure campaign language – a call to protest, to take action against a reprehensible company, later referred to as 'obnoxious'. We therefore read the first line with the expectations of having this reinforced and indeed highly emotive language – 'threatening to destroy' – is found here. The propaganda wheels are turning in our heads, as we make associations with other such texts we've come across in the past. The language continually plays on this style – 'We appeal to your conscience', 'our struggle', 'Our entire existence', 'We urge you' – all lexis normally found in genuine propaganda material. It's only after we've read a substantial amount, and taken time to think about it, that the penny drops – we're meant to do the total opposite: not boycott but patronise and take advantage of these 'outrageous' prices. It's a very sophisticated and clever form of advertising and even adds the small print at the bottom, urging us not to drop this leaflet on the street. Needless to say, that's exactly what the company wants you to do, to spread the word, and, in fact, that's exactly how the leaflets were distributed.

Text: House of Happiness

Commentary

This Alliance and Leicester advert dresses up the rather mundane issue of mortgages by taking a very familiar format – that of the old Hollywood horror movie poster. As discussed in Unit 3, graphics and print style are important aspects and here the horror is represented by the wobbly lettering, the image of the house on the hill (reminiscent of the *Psycho* film) and the expressions of the couple. But the purpose is not to terrify, nor to appeal to the horror-crazed, but to turn those associations on their head. So the couple's expression is toned down from the horror-struck and 'the title' is changed from 'House of Horrors' to 'House of Happiness' – the opposite meaning while retaining the alliterative phrasing. The positioning of the text is also reminiscent of such movie posters, with a lead in at the top, catchy promises ('Full of horrors' becoming '<u>No</u> horrors!') and the lower corner telling us the 'starring' attractions. The text at the bottom begins with a passing attempt to allude to the theme, referring to 'the monster mortgage' but then moves into highly conventional style and language, common to small print details of such companies.

Commentary

Now look at the Text: Window problems opposite. The Coldseal advertising campaign is based on the reader's knowledge of the layout and design of newspaper editorials. The effect works across the whole page rather than with a conventional, single ad – but that's there too, in the lower right-hand corner, reinforcing the impression at first glance that the rest of the page is *non*-advertising. With columns and borders, it would appear that each piece is a separate article written by different reporters, although if we look closely, only two reporters are cited. If we begin reading this article, we're led to believe this is a consumer-interest article, reporting generally on different double glazing companies ('So many double glazing companies use high pressure sales tactics') and giving advice ('If you're thinking of replacing your windows, here is some important advice'). In fact, the overall appeal is to the consumer's concerns and implies a caring company, looking out for the consumer's best interests ('Advice corner', 'Be safe not sorry', 'Worried about security . . .?'). It isn't until the second column that the advertising company, Coldseal, is mentioned by name but it's still presented as if by an outsider of the company – 'you should consider a company like Coldseal. At Coldseal . . .'. Missing here are the inclusive pronouns ('We at Coldseal . . .') or deixis ('Here at Coldseal . . .'). Of course, the heading 'Advertisement feature' does appear in the top right-hand corner but that's

Text: Window problems

WINDOW PROBLEMS?

Be safe not sorry

■ **Choose a company with a good reputation**

IN 2000 we are all aware of the rising crime figures, many people are starting to look carefully at how they secure their property.

Security is obviously of great importance when choosing replacement windows and doors.

Many products being offered may not be as secure as you have been lead to believe and in actual fact, some replacement windows are less safe than the original frames.

Secure

Insist that the product you choose has been specifically designed to ensure security for your home and prized possessions. Basically, this type of system is self-locking, meaning that when installed the windows and doors are virtually burglar proof. Choose a company with a good reputation and make sure that the products are designed with security in mind.

Coldseal is a local company that offers just this. Every window that leaves Coldseal has a turn-key locking handle with an indicator to show whether it is locked or not, an anti-theft high security locking wedge and gasket. All Coldseal doors have a specially designed locking system with multipoint locks and reinforced panels or toughened glass as standard.

If you would like a truly honest quotation for your home improvements, contact the professionals, Coldseal on freephone 0800 221155.

You cannot replace your possessions, but you can replace your windows with secure products from Coldseal!

ADVICE

Check whether the window you're considering has a security guarantee

corner

Stop now - before you spend your hard-earned cash

Report by Steve Thompson

IF you're thinking of replacing your windows, here is some important advice. Before you enter into the very competitive double glazing minefield, be sure you know what you want to purchase and be positive on the amount you wish to spend. So many double glazing companies use high pressure sales tactics, that it is so easy to get carried away.

Always get more than one quote. Nobody can tell you which company to choose, but here is some very important and valuable advice when obtaining quotations for work to be done.

Be careful to choose the right quality (beware - all PVC-U windows are not the same). Visit or inspect an installation before you decide. Try to speak to a previous customer. Do not pay any extras or listen to any crazy discounts - 60% off can't be believable nor 'Buy One Get One Free' - and always ask for a final price before considering.

Having read all the above, you should consider a company like Coldseal.

At Coldseal there are NO hard sales tactics - just hard-working staff and service with a smile.

Everything that leaves the factories is made to the highest standards. To arrange a quotation telephone Coldseal, the local company that cares on freephone 0800 221155.

When you are spending your hard earned cash beware that you spend it wisely.

The Coldseal aim is to fit top quality windows made to the highest standards at comparable prices to those quoted by other local companies and national competitors.

The effect of this is to build up trust and reliability with valued customers and future business will be built solely on customer recommendations. The Coldseal pledge is: Give people quality and value for money. Our customers' recommendation is so important to our reputation.

Coldseal have an impressive, hi-tech manufacturing facility to ensure that your windows are produced to exacting quality, and then fitted by trained teams. Coldseal operate local Customer Service Centres to support their valued customers if required to do so with helpful advice.

Coldseal is fast becoming the largest window company in the UK due to this outstanding service.

■ **Worried about security from your windows?**

Spreading the word

THE oldest saying in the world of selling is that the best advert is a happy customer.

Every day the national window company Coldseal receive letters from satisfied customers who are not only happy but also relieved because let's face it, the double glazing industry has had its share of bad publicity and no one really knows about the Coldseal difference until they've had their installation completed.

When Coldseal set up in business many years ago, they set out to offer their customers a level of service that did away with all the negative things that customers disliked about buying windows and only offer them the things they liked. Written guarantees, optional maintenance, competitive payment plans, and importantly above all complete confidence.

Ask anyone of the many thousands of happy customers who have had a Coldseal installation and they'll tell you . . . Coldseal really are different from other window companies. . . and that's another promise Coldseal will keep! Coldseal enhance your home with top quality products, good guarantees and top customer service.

Thinking of replacing those old draughty window frames?

By Rachel Jordon

AWARD-WINNING window giant Coldseal has rocked the industry once again by throwing out the traditional image of the double-glazing business and replacing it with the best quality, service and value that money can buy. This window company is even saying NO to customers...

NO charge for finding out more - Coldseal carry out free initial advice and free surveys to help you reach the right decision - even calling them is free - 0800 221155.

NO high pressure selling tactics.

NO risk - written guarantees of both product specification and installation workmanship given to customers before order is placed.

NO 'off the shelf' windows - custom made PVC-U frames manufactured in their own factory to your exact specification just for your home.

NO unwelcome visitors - Coldseal windows and doors offer a robust response to the problem of domestic burglary by specifying often unique and patented locking devices and many design features that combine to help beat the would-be thief.

NO 'get rich quick and disappear tactics' - a ten-year after sales commitment. This approach is just another indication of Coldseal's commitment to long-term customer care.

State of the art computerised local customer services centres are staffed by experienced operators who will offer help or advice on any aspect of your installation. It is important to Coldseal that you receive good service, so they can say: 'No-one else is in the frame'. In the new millennium the companies that will succeed will be the companies like Coldseal, that people trust.

■ **Are your windows old and rotten like these?**

NEW millennium no better time to buy

COLDSEAL Limited have introduced a new Goldcard account which is available to make the purchase of PVC-U windows, doors and conservatories easy. You have the freedom to make payments which enables you to take advantage of the fact that windows are cheaper now than in the past and give the benefit of a double indemnity guarantee from Coldseal for up to 10 years.

We recommend you take advantage of these facilities you should ring Coldseal free on 0800 221155. The Goldcard account gives you the freedom for you to decide how to arrange your finances and is backed by a major national bank.

net.benefits
www.coldseal.co.uk

STOP!

Do not buy a window, door or conservatory until you call free on

0800 22 11 55

COLDSEAL

NO-ONE ELSE IS IN THE FRAME

easily missed in the context of the newspaper as a whole and when the name and date appear normally in larger print at the very top.

Spoken texts which don't fit the mould

We've discussed spoken texts which involve interaction, such as conversation, and those which are monologues, in story-telling or lecturing. The distinction here seems clear-cut and each displays different language features. Once again, however, there are texts which are not absolutely one thing or another.

Activity

Look at the Text: Effective language teaching and try to decide what kind of text it is. What language features are characteristic of such a text?

Text: Effective language teaching

Imagine a teacher coming into the classroom and telling the class, 'Now today we're going to learn about flowers and here are all the technical terms you'll need.' She then writes up on the board words like stamen, pistil and stalk, gives the definition and says to the class, 'Learn all this off by heart and until you do, you won't see a single, real flower.'

Now, of course, no one would teach like that. Rather, more likely, the teacher would come in, armed with a bunch of flowers. They'd be given out and the children would start looking at the parts. 'What's this bit called, miss?' one would ask and the teacher would mention the technical names as need arose.

The parallel with grammar teaching is plain. In the old days, the teacher came in, wrote some artificial sentences up on the board and made the children learn the technical names by heart. Today, the teacher is likely to come in, armed with real language in the form of advertisements, news reports, scientific documents, tapes of news broadcasts and dozens of other examples of English in use. The class talks about what's going on and why the language is effective or fails to be effective and the technical terms are brought into the discussion along the way.

Commentary

This is a transcript of a talk given by the linguist David Crystal on a BBC Radio 4 programme in the series *English Now*. It's a scripted lecture and therefore designed as a written text to be read aloud. It's within the lecture genre but we could sub-divide this genre into political, professional, academic and popular and place this text in the sub-genre category of popular-academic. It assumes a fairly educated audience, interested in grammar, but is not aimed at university graduates, for example. This has implications for the type of lexis used, the register and style.

There are many types of texts, like this, which are written in order to be read aloud: lectures, TV idiot boards, news broadcasts, speeches. They lack the features of spontaneous spoken discourse with its false starts, hesitations and repetitions. In fact, this is the main area in which scripted dialogue for TV and movies lacks authenticity, for although you might get the odd pause, you rarely get slips of the tongue, false starts and general fluffing. You can see any out-take programme where these have been cut out of the final transmission, seen as poorly delivered rather than realistic. For more formal speeches, this is precisely the reason for the prepared script – to allow for fluency, accuracy, lack of ambiguity and professional delivery. (When you hear some of the terrible gaffs politicians and members of royalty make when they deviate from a script to make off-the-cuff remarks, you can see why the script is so important.)

However, listening at length to a totally scripted and rehearsed speech places a tremendous burden on the audience due to the different nature of the spoken and written medium – written discourse is designed to be read, spoken to be heard. As one crosses over to the other, if language features fail to get adapted in the process, problems arise.

Activity

Compare the scripted radio broadcast version above with the Text: Grammatical nature rambles? produced by the same author on the same topic but now as a printed version which was published in *The Cambridge Encyclopedia of Language*. What differences between the two versions can you detect which seem to reflect the more spoken nature of the first (albeit scripted) and the written nature of the second?

Text: Grammatical nature rambles?

> Imagine teaching a child about the structure of a flower in the following way.
> A hypothetical plant is drawn on the board, and its parts labelled: stamen,
> pistil, stalk, etc. Each term is defined, and the children write them in their
> books. They have to learn them off by heart, and until they do they will *not*
> be allowed to see or work with any real plant!
>
> It is unlikely that anyone in a modern biology class would be taught this
> topic through such an approach. The teacher would arrive armed with real
> plants, and give them out; then the children would search for the parts, all
> the while meeting problems, and asking for help with the labels as they went
> along. Later, the teacher would get them to write up their project in a book,
> and then might ask for some terms to be learned.
>
> That is the modern way: discovery first, definitions of terms last. But
> grammar continues to suffer, in many schools, by being taught the other way
> round (when it is taught at all!). A hypothetical sentence is put on the board,
> and the required grammatical terminology has to be learned, before any
> attempt is made to grapple with real sentences in a real world. Often, even,
> no attempt at all is made to go searching for interesting, real, sentence
> specimens. It is as if the children's knowledge of plants were to remain forever
> solely on the blackboard. No one would tolerate such a silly pedagogical
> approach for biology. But for many decades, just such an approach was
> actively practised for grammar – and it is by no means extinct.

Commentary

The structure of the texts is the same: an imaginary situation is described
before a real, or more likely, scenario is presented. Both address the
reader/listener directly ('Imagine . . .'). In the scripted text, Crystal has a
more positive attitude towards current grammar teaching, whereas in the
written text he sounds far more critical that bad practice still persists.

Some language comparisons

◉   The second text is more impersonal than the first. This is achieved by
    use of the **passive** ('A hypothetical plant <u>is drawn</u>', 'Each term <u>is
    defined</u>') and by using **impersonal nouns** which avoid the mention
    of a human agent ('teaching <u>a child</u>', 'through such <u>an approach</u>').

- The first text is much more anecdotal, using direct speech to make it sound more lively and real ('What's this bit called, miss?').
- There is ellipsis ('Rather more likely . . .') in the first text but none in the second.
- The second text makes use of italics and punctuation ('they will *not* be allowed to see or work with any real plant!') to represent stress whereas, although not reproduced here, in the first text the speaker made use of a full range of prosodic features to convey meaning and attitude: intonation, pace and stress.

You can also consider sentence length, formality, modality, connectives, and so on, but you need to remember that a scripted spoken text occupies middle ground between a spontaneous oral commentary and a written-to-be-read-silently text.

Texts with features of both writing and speaking

We've looked at written texts which don't conform to all the conventions of writing yet remain in essence written texts. We've looked at spoken texts which don't conform to all the conventions of speaking yet remain in essence spoken texts. There is still one more category to cover – texts which contain elements of both. (A linguistic joke would be to invent a new name and call them 'bi-textuals' and then the elements that cross from one medium to another could be called 'trans-textuals' – but those aren't official linguistic terms – yet – so we'd better forget about them for the moment.)

Activity

The following text appeared in a newspaper. It's obviously a written text but it uses the format of an oral interview. We don't know if the interviewee was asked to write down her answers or if this is supposed to be a transcript from a recording. If it is the latter, some things don't quite ring true. From the interview, which language features seem to reflect a written style and which spoken?

Text: First impressions

First impressions are vital for receptionist on the front line

MAUREEN Lawrence is married and works as a receptionist and sales administrator. She has been in this role for nine months.

Briefly describe your job

I am the first person that people meet when they contact the company. I man the main phone lines, taking enquires down and dealing with the more minor ones.

I greet visitors when they come into the building and escort them to the place where they need to be. I need to be dressed appropriately all the time.

What hours do you work?

9am to 5.30pm, five days a week.

What do you enjoy most?

I most enjoy the fact that I work in a very lively office, so the atmosphere is always buzzing.

My job is varied, changing from day-to-day so I don't get bored. I enjoy meeting new people as well.

What do you least enjoy?

Sometimes after a *very* manic period it gets a bit quiet so that can be a bit boring.

I am the type of person who always needs something to do!

What interested you in the first place and how did you get into this job?

I was made redundant from a sales job in a different area of the country with the same group.

I looked for another job internally and found this vacancy.

What personal qualities and qualifications and what training did you need?

I needed to have some experience in the radio industry as the work involves dealing with jargon.

MAUREEN Lawrence: She enjoys a buzzing atmosphere.

I undertook some IT training, which I have now completed, to bring myself up-to-date with the software that the company uses.

You need to have a good phone manner and personal presentation skills are very important.

What opportunities are there for development and promotion?

Because the group is nationwide there are a lot of opportunities to move around internally and also around the country.

What is the salary range from trainee to senior rank?

Trainees start at around £7,500 and the job's top salary I should think is around £15k.

What other benefits are there (company car, pension etc)?

The company has a pension scheme and a profit share scheme for all employees.

What is your ambition?

For the moment I am content where I am so I suppose my ambition is just to stay happy with my life.

CONTACT: The Chartered Institute of Secretaries and Administrators on – 0171 580 4741.

Commentary

Some examples of language features which seem to reflect a written or a spoken style are shown in Table 6.1. Note also the graphological attempts to represent phonological features, such as the use of italics to convey stress ('*very* manic') and the exclamation mark to convey a rather difficult attitude to paraphrase but something like, 'I know you'll think that funny or odd'.

Table 6.1 Written and spoken features

	Written	*Spoken*
grammar	non-contractions – 'I am', 'My job is'	use of first person – 'I greet', 'I need'
	formal linking: gerund – 'I man', 'taking'; relative clauses – 'which I have now'; word order – 'I most enjoy'	repeated structures – 'I am the first person', 'I man', 'I greet'; short answer forms – '9 am to 5.30pm'
lexis	some formal – 'to be dressed appropriately', 'I undertook'	colloquial and informal – 'buzzing', 'manic', 'a bit', 'I suppose'; vague language – 'at around £7,500', 'I should think is around £15k'
discourse	structured, controlled 'answers' to the 'questions' which develop at length without further prompting	question/answer exchanges with more than one 'voice'

Written dialogue

One very common area where we're used to reading spoken language in print is in literary writing. Drama is usually, of course, predominantly dialogue. Stage directions and background details are usually minimal.

We've said that literary texts tend to create their own context; they're fairly self-contained. For this reason, we don't normally question the format and language chosen by the author. If we do, it's normally because something in the process hasn't worked properly. We accept what we find in a literary text and assume that everything there is according to the purposeful design of the writer.

Classic dramatic dialogue

If a drama has stretches of poetical dialogue, we see it either as part of the time in which the text was created or as a feature of the individual writer's style. We don't criticise it for not being the spoken language of current everyday conversation. For example, Shakespeare's first dialogue exchange between Romeo and Juliet is as follows:

> ROMEO [*To Juliet*] If I profane with my unworthiest hand
> This holy shrine, the gentle sin is this;
> My lips, two blushing pilgrims, ready stand
> To smooth that rough touch with a tender kiss.
> JULIET Good pilgrim, you do wrong your hand too much
> Which mannerly devotion shows in this;
> For saints have hands that pilgrims' hands do touch,
> And palm to palm is holy palmers' kiss.
>
> (*Romeo and Juliet*, Act 1, Scene V,
> lines 97–104)

Even in Elizabethan England, people didn't walk around speaking in verse to each other. To prove it, take the opening of this scene where the servants are scurrying around preparing for the ball in the hall of the Capulets' house:

> FIRST SERVINGMAN Where's Potpan, that he helps not to take away? he shift a trencher! he scrape a trencher!
>
> (ibid. lines 1–3)

Shakespeare, for the most part, reserves poetical language for dialogue between main characters on non-trivial themes; the daily toing and froing of everyday conversation is expressed in prose. The language style chosen, therefore, reflects the characters and the event or plot. It's a conscious decision. Realism isn't always, if ever, the issue. If the prose dialogue is realistic *enough* for the audience to be able to identify with the characters and to know what's going on, the writer has achieved one part of his or her purpose. The verse dialogue has an extra dimension, that of the language itself. Carefully crafted in terms of sounds, rhyme, rhythm and lexis, aesthetic qualities overlay the language of the dialogue. But it isn't a poem, in the voice of the poet. The voice has to be that of the character and reflect aspects of that character's personality.

Modern dramatic dialogue

Times, fashions and styles change. At one time, literary writing needed to conform to fairly rigid conventions. Today, for many literary writers, anything goes. Again, the purpose is a crucial factor. Is the dramatic writer trying to reflect real life? Is the purpose to teach a moral, raise awareness, make us laugh?

Purists might argue that TV scripts aren't 'literature' at all. You can see that the word 'literature' hasn't been used here but rather 'literary texts', as there tend to be images and expectations created in people's minds by that word. Certainly, taking extracts out of context, it might be hard to distinguish a TV script from a conventionally accepted dramatic work.

Activity

The following extract is taken from a script of a TV sitcom called *Father Ted*, shown on British television's Channel 4 in the mid-1990s. How does the language here compare with that of Shakespeare? What does the language reflect here?

Text: Father Ted

SCENE | 4 INT. DAY
SET | HALLWAY – PAROCHIAL HOUSE^
STUDIO

TED: What are we going to do!? Think, Dougal, think!

(DOUGAL LOOKS VERY BLANK.)

TED: OK, I'll do the thinking. God, what'll we do?

DOUGAL: Ted. . . . Jack.

TED: Oh, God, if he sees him! He'll . . . Christ almighty! I'll have to break it to him gently. You get Paul out of the house and I'll –

DOUGAL: You're not leaving me alone with him, Ted!

Commentary

Realism now *is* an issue. A conscious attempt has been made to make the dialogue sound authentic. It seems to be close to normal everyday speech. There are short utterances, exclamations and injunctions, pauses ('He'll . . . Christ almighty!') and unfinished remarks ('and I'll –'). There are, however, no false starts, no slips and no repetitions. So it's realistic enough but, if it contained all the features of normal speech, the dialogue would be slowed down, it might become more difficult to follow and it would risk making the audience think the actors had slipped up. That would be devastating for performance drama which tries to sustain illusion; it doesn't want to wake the audience up into the real world and draw attention to the performance itself.

Dialogue in fiction

Very few works of fiction have no dialogue at all. It's usually felt essential for breaking the monotony of lengthy prose sections. More importantly, most writers feel it's the ideal vehicle for revealing the personalities of their characters. Popular guides on how to write fiction advise using dialogue rather than lengthy character descriptions but classical writers have always tended to keep to this principle. In fictional works, dialogue is nearly always framed within sections of prose text. The writer then has to employ a variety of techniques for changing style, for bringing in the dialogue and for adding tags ('she said', 'he groaned') where necessary.

Activity

Read the following extract, which covers the first meeting, apart from a brief introduction earlier, of the main characters in the story whose relationship forms one of the central themes of the book.

Text: *The Horse Whisperer*

'Hello, Joe. How are you?'
'Good.'
She looked up the valley, toward the mountains, then looked back at Tom.
'What a beautiful place.'
'It is.'
He was wondering when she was going to get around to saying what on earth she was doing here, though he already had an idea. She took a deep breath.
'Mr Booker, you're going to think this is insane, but you can probably guess why I've come here.'

'Well. I kind of reckoned you didn't just happen to be passing through.' She almost smiled.

'I'm sorry just turning up like this, but I knew what you'd say if I phoned. It's about my daughter's horse.'

'Pilgrim.'

'Yes. I know you can help him and I came here to ask you, to beg you, to have another look at him.'

'Mrs Graves . . .'

'Please. Just a look. It wouldn't take long.'

Tom laughed. 'What, to fly to New York?' He nodded at the Lariat. 'Or were you counting on driving me there?'

'He's here. In Choteau.'

Tom stared at her for a moment in disbelief.

'You've hauled him all the way out here?' She nodded. Joe was looking from one of them to the other, trying to get the picture. Diane had stepped out onto the porch and stood there holding open the screen door, watching.

'All on your own?' Tom asked.

'With Grace, my daughter.'

Commentary

Again there are features of spoken discourse which you should be familiar with by now. Participants take turns and some turns form adjacency pairs ('How are you?' / 'Good'). Not all the turns are of equal length – in this section, Annie has the longest turns, as she's the one initiating the conversation and making the request. The first part of the conversation follows conventional opening routines with phatic exchanges ('What a beautiful place.' / 'It is'). The vocabulary is informal and sentences are short. Contractions are used and in some utterances, ellipsis ('Just a look', 'What, to fly to New York?').

There is also overlap at one point, as Tom's utterance remains unfinished as Annie interjects ('Mrs Graves . . .' / 'Please'). Once again, though, the false starts and slips don't appear. (The reformulated 'I came here to ask you, to beg you' is more a case of emphasis than a false start.)

Nevertheless, the dialogue has the right kind of feel; there's nothing so artificial as to draw the reader's attention to it; it is *sufficiently realistic*.

The author doesn't need to do more because, as it stands, it conveys the tension of this first meeting in which, apart from the normal awkwardness of first meetings, Annie is nervous in anticipating Tom's refusal to help. It does more than this though – with the length of Annie's turns, we get a picture of her dominant, confident character, set in contrast to the shorter turns to reflect Tom Booker's taciturn, ironic view of life.

On a cline of literariness, similar to those in Unit 5, this novel would not be at the furthest point; some authors might have handled the dialogue more skilfully, conveying the emotions which are here made explicit in the text ('sheepish', 'disbelief') solely through dialogue. However, it illustrates the point that dialogue in fiction has ulterior motives, which don't exist in normal conversation, and therefore doesn't necessarily replicate real-life speech down to the last detail. Dialogue in fiction, above all else, is intended to be *read* by a *reader* who is being made to feel like a silent third party. Some sacrifices therefore have to be made.

Effects of technology

Another area where we find language occupying a middle ground is that associated with modern technology. Technology develops so quickly that things are in place before we, the users, really know what to do with them. We bring to a new medium the strategies and techniques we already use and then adapt them as and when necessary. They may need discarding altogether in favour of something totally new. This then means that there's a period of time where things are still in a state of flux – 'the jury's still out' on what's the best way to deal with things.

This is the state of play at the moment with answering service messages, email messages, interactive real-time electronic exchanges and mobile phone text messages. The physical, concrete means of transmission always has a tremendous influence on the communication itself. Just think of the differences of writing with a quill pen, a fountain pen, a biro, a typewriter, an early word processor, a computer, electronic messaging.

The pace at which language can be produced and the correction facilities available will affect and subsequently determine the type of communication and the language used. You've probably noticed yourself that work you compose directly on to the computer will be completely different from work you produce free-hand.

Today, time is of the essence – socially, professionally and personally. People are racing around much faster than ever before and we identified in Unit 5 that speed and urgency influence the choice of medium and the language employed. This means that if time or cost is a factor, communication has to be speedy, time- and cost-efficient and this means reducing it to the bare essentials. Thus, we can distinguish between two types of effects: graphic and interpersonal.

Graphic

To send a text message by mobile phone where charges may be incurred per character, money can be saved by replacing words with single letters or figures. Similarly with the Internet, particularly with IRC (Internet Relay Chat – real time, online chat), where people have said their reasons for cutting things down are low online speed, poor typing skills and the need for quick responses. Thus 'See you later' can be sent in emails and mobile phone text messages as 'CUL8R' or even 'L8R'. 'Nething' which can be shortened will be:

> UR
> 2moro
> –er>a (dinna)
> gr8

So spelling gets distorted but it has to be systematic for people to understand it and one easy way is to revert to phonetic spelling.

Symbols and punctuation marks can be used to represent moods, as with emoticons (emotional icons):

> :-) happy, smiling
> ;-) winking
> :-(frowning, sad
> :'-(crying

Interpersonal

If time and money are major considerations, then the fundamental human desire for conducting interpersonal communication has to carry on in a new form. The six-page long epistle sent cross-country by horse gives way to the hour-long telephone call gives way to

 Well done!

113

Although *The Rough Guide to the Internet* makes the point that emoticons are 'only meant to be fun :-)' (Kennedy, 1999, p.458), the fact is that they are becoming a communication system in themselves and are one method of conveying emotion within the written medium which would otherwise be more difficult and time-consuming. As with any 'language', it's a question of knowledge, learning and applying appropriately. And, as with any other form of knowledge, people who are not 'in the know' tend to get frightened. This is not necessarily an age issue but, due to the rapid technological rise, a gulf, which will reduce with time, does at present exist between those 'in and not in the know'. However, due to the nature of technology itself, there's also a gulf between the 'technowhizz' and the 'technophobe'. What's interesting to speculate is how much a passing fad this notational trend is and how limited or exploitable it proves to be.

Time and money

As such forms of telecommunications are still in their relative infancy, it's impossible to know how things will develop. We can only look at the current state of affairs and note that time and money are highly influential factors.

The question of economy isn't quite so relevant for the email message sender who can usually compose off-line at no cost but time is still likely to be a factor. Much of the nature of such communications, certainly for the private user, is interpersonal. We're keeping up contact with distant relatives and friends, showing that we're thinking of them and using the form, for the most part, in place of conventional letters.

If we're in a hurry, and we share the code with our participants, whole words and phrases can be represented by their initial letters:

AFAIK   as far as I know
BTW   by the way
BRB   be right back
IYSWIM   if you see what I mean

This kind of shorthand is hardly new: in many contexts, initials have commonly been used to refer to institutions and companies and so on (NBC, EU, MA) but in emails, initials are used to convey incidental expressions which occur again and again and are much more related to the interpersonal nature of communication than to physical facts.

It's not just the fact that we might be in a hurry that we use a fairly quick and informal style. It's the immediacy of the send/receive mode, not only with IRC but with conventional emailing that affects the language and style. Because of the speed of response, it's very close to a verbal conversation and resembles it in its often chatty, colloquial style. At the same time, we can't ignore the constraints imposed by the channel: mentally planning and composing, typing, seeing the words in print are all part of the writing process but this immediate communication event doesn't easily lend itself to a more formal written style. Hangovers from conventional letter writing still persist for many users, so some people feel unsure whether to start with Dear Bob or just Bob or Hi, Hi-ja . . . or nothing at all. There has always been a problem with writing that humour might not come across. Before modern printing methods, writers were restricted mainly to such things as exclamation marks to overcome this problem. Now the much wider range of symbols and punctuation marks that we've looked at can be used to the same purpose.

Activity

Look at the following email messages and chat room contributions. Study the use of language first of all and then compare the use of symbols, punctuation, abbreviations, spelling, capitalisation and so on.

Text: Emails 1

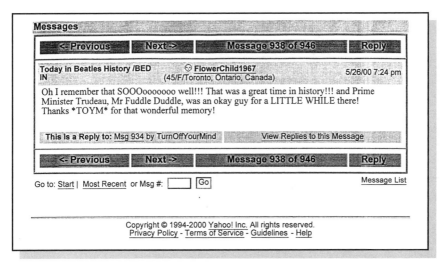

continued

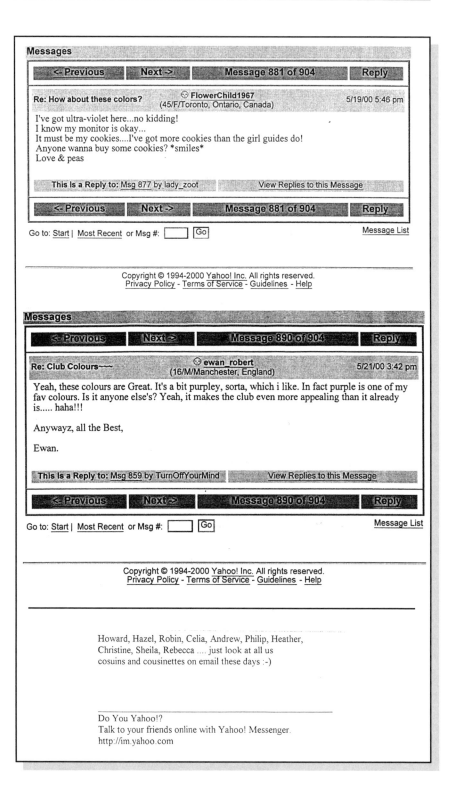

Messages

Re: How about these colors?   ☺ FlowerChild1967   5/19/00 5:46 pm
(45/F/Toronto, Ontario, Canada)

I've got ultra-violet here...no kidding!
I know my monitor is okay...
It must be my cookies....I've got more cookies than the girl guides do!
Anyone wanna buy some cookies? *smiles*
Love & peas

This Is a Reply to: Msg 877 by lady_zoot   View Replies to this Message

<- Previous   Next ->   Message 881 of 904   Reply

Go to: Start | Most Recent or Msg #: [____] [Go]   Message List

Messages

Re: Club Colours~~~   ☺ ewan_robert   5/21/00 3:42 pm
(16/M/Manchester, England)

Yeah, these colours are Great. It's a bit purpley, sorta, which i like. In fact purple is one of my fav colours. Is it anyone else's? Yeah, it makes the club even more appealing than it already is..... haha!!!

Anywayz, all the Best,

Ewan.

This Is a Reply to: Msg 859 by TurnOffYourMind   View Replies to this Message

<- Previous   Next ->   Message 890 of 904   Reply

Go to: Start | Most Recent or Msg #: [____] [Go]   Message List

Howard, Hazel, Robin, Celia, Andrew, Philip, Heather,
Christine, Sheila, Rebecca .... just look at all us
cosuins and cousinettes on email these days :-)

Do You Yahoo!?
Talk to your friends online with Yahoo! Messenger.
http://im.yahoo.com

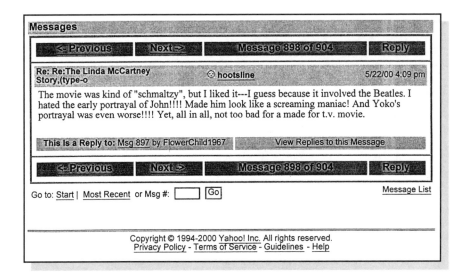

Activity

The two emails in Text: Emails 2 have been sent between Rebecca and her mum. They provide a close point of contrast to highlight some of the features we've discussed so far. Compare the two.

Text: Emails 2

Hi!
How did you manage to get your own email account type thing? How can I get one?! hope you're well and enjoy Telford etc speak to you soon
love Beccah

ps. would you like me to get you a pair of CK flared bootcut type jeans? If so what size? – They're only $24.99!!!!!

> Hi Rebecca,
> I have ordered the two books from the
> library, they should be here by the time you
> get back. You can borrow them for three
> weeks, I think you will be able to renew
> them after that. I was thinking we might
> give you a ring tomorrow (Saturday).
>
> That's all for now.
> Love Mum xxx
> P.S. You can now send mail to Joanna at
> her new address.

117

Commentary

If we drew a cline of more to less email chattiness, similar to those in Unit 5, we'd find Rebecca and her mum quite far apart. Something like this:

- ◎ Openings – Rebecca uses 'Hi' with an exclamation mark and no name. Her mum also uses 'Hi' but adds the full name and a conventional letter greeting comma.
- ◎ Vague language – Rebecca's informal style includes vague terms ('email account type thing') whereas her mum is more definite ('two books', 'three weeks').
- ◎ Punctuation – Rebecca uses some punctuation marks in conventional ways, such as the question marks, dash and apostrophe, but uses the exclamation mark to convey how impressed she is ('How can I get one?!'). Although there are some capital letters, others are omitted (notably on '*love* Beccah'), as are some full stops. Her mum, on the other hand, uses more conventional punctuation though with some use of commas instead of full-stops. Capitalisation is more consistent and is used, traditionally, in the closing. Also compare the postscript lettering, punctuation and capitalisation in both.
- ◎ Contractions – more frequent in Rebecca's message while her mum uses full forms, apart from when signing off.
- ◎ Ellipsis – only occurs in Rebecca's message ([I] 'hope you're well').

From this comparison, it can be seen that email messages, like the other texts we've looked at in this unit, cross the boundaries between spoken and written language but not in a uniform, fixed way. There are many different variations as there are differing individual styles and preferences.

Conclusion

Throughout the book, we've looked at texts both written and spoken. Although the texts have been widely different, they've all had something in common i.e. they are all *texts*. So here's a riddle to end on: When is a text not a text?

Look at this:

sincere omen sour voice over
excess ransom case minor answer vain exercise
wire sons vain error
unwise cream remove
nervous manner immune over unanimous war
immense snow came near arrow use
nice women rave cocoa essence
scan access river oarsmen view
muse waxes over iron sawn ream vows

Question: What is it? Is it a text?

Answer: It's a sight-reading chart from an optician's surgery, devised purely to test eye-sight.

So the solution to the riddle, 'When is a text not a text?' is that a text is not a text if there is no cohesion or coherence. In order to convey meaning, there must be at least coherence; without it, we don't convey meaning and therefore there is no text, no communication taking place.

However, it's a sign of the innate human quality of co-operation that we assume someone is trying to convey meaning and we struggle to identify it. It's even possible to find some, if we try hard enough.

In this unit, and hopefully throughout the development of the book, we've found that nothing is ever quite as simple as it first appears. Most of us have such vast experience of so many different types of both written and spoken texts that that range can be exploited to the full for various purposes. Advertisers, literary authors and humorists have the full field to play with. Many of the strict rules and fixed boundaries of an earlier age have broken down or been pushed to their limits. Language today knows very few bounds, not only for professional writers but for all language users. This is as it should be – language is dynamic, living, ever-changing. The main point is that we should convey our messages as intended and that we are understood as planned.

The choices are ours: to write or to speak and, once that decision has been made, we choose the language most appropriate to our needs and purposes. If we remain aware of those choices, then when we are on the receiving end of language, acting as co-participants in language exchanges, we should be more alert as to the messages being directed at us. In that way, we should be able to interpret messages successfully and not be unduly swayed by those seeking to persuade or influence us.

Extension

1   There are many examples of multi-layered adverts in papers and magazines such as those on pp. 98 and 99. Find one and, if possible, find an authentic example of the other text type on which its appeal is based. Compare the versions in detail.

2   You're going to interview somebody who works in the place where you study or someone else you know who has a job (a neighbour, friend of the family, etc.). You're going to tape-record the interview and then transcribe part of it afterwards. First of all divide into two groups. Half the group should plan and write down the interview questions. The other half of the group should *not* make any notes but of course you'll need to give some thought to the sort of things you're going to ask. The idea is to compare afterwards the differences between a structured, controlled interview and a more spontaneous conversation. Finally, compare the results with the Maureen Lawrence interview on p. 106.

3   What symbols and abbreviations do you use or have you seen in e-mails and mobile phone text messages? Could you categorise them by what you think is meant by 'graphic' as opposed to 'interpersonal'?

4   The newspapers are full of reports and readers' letters about the decline of language and that emails etc. are destroying literacy skills and the 'art of communication'. Discuss your views on this either in the form of an oral debate or as a written argument.

5   Analyse some email exchanges and mobile phone text messages of your own or your friends. Look for both the written word and the use of symbols and abbreviations. Do proportions vary and, if so, why?

6   Either find, or compose, two email messages which would fit the two extreme ends of the cline on p. 118, i.e. one very informal, more than Rebecca's, and one very formal, more than her mum's. Compare the features of all four messages.

7   Try to find other examples of texts which seem to cross the boundaries between written and spoken language. Spread the range across the popular press, academic texts, literature and so on. (There are some very innovative modern books/plays/poems which

deliberately exploit the boundary issue.) Analyse the language closely according to differences we've highlighted in this and previous units.

index of terms

This is a form of combined glossary and index. Listed below are some of the main key terms used in the book, together with brief definitions for purposes of reference. The page references will normally take you to the first use of the term in the book, where it is shown in bold.

accent 30
> The ways in which words are pronounced. Accent can vary according to the region or social class of a speaker.

adjacency pair 64
> Adjacency pairs are parallel expressions used across the boundaries of individual speaking turns. They are usually ritualistic and formulaic socially. For example, 'Good morning'/'Good morning' or 'How are things?'/'Fine thanks' or 'Congratulations'/'Thanks'.

anaphoric reference 9
> (see **reference**)

back-channel 65
> Words, phrases and non-verbal utterances (e.g. 'I see', 'oh', 'uhhuh', 'really', 'erm') used by a listener to give feedback to a speaker that the message is being followed and understood.

cline 81
> A term used to express the way in which features or language are not absolutes but operate along a gradient or continuum of effects. For example, there is a cline from spoken to written language or from informal to formal interactions.

cohesive device 7
> Cohesive devices are words and grammatical structures which provide links across clause and sentence boundaries so that a text reads in a logically connected and coherent way.

deixis 62
> Words such as 'this', 'that', 'here', 'there' which refer backwards or forwards or which point outside a specific text are normally referred to as the main deictic expressions.

delexical verbs 63
> Delexical verbs are verbal phrases such as 'have a swim', 'have a sleep', 'get a drink' which are more common in spoken and informal usage than the individual verbs (swim, sleep and drink) from which they are formed.

dialect 30
> The distinctive grammar and vocabulary which is associated with a regional or social use of a language.

discourse markers 65
> Words and phrases which are used to signal the relationships and connections between utterances and to signpost that what is said can be followed by the listener or reader. For example, 'first', 'on the other hand',

'now', 'you know', 'you see', 'what's more' are all discourse markers. Some discourse markers are more likely to be used in spoken discourse than in written discourse and vice versa.

ellipsis 62

Ellipsis refers to the omission of part of a grammatical structure. For example, in the sentence, 'She went to the party and danced all night' the pronoun 'she' is ellipted from the second clause. In the dialogue:

'You going to the party?'
'Might be.'

the verb 'are' and the pronoun 'I' are, respectively, omitted. The resulting ellipsis conveys a more casual and informal tone.

filler 61

Words or sounds in spontaneous speech such as 'er', 'sort of', 'I mean', 'well' which do not carry any conventional meaning but which allow a speaker time to think and to pre-plan an utterance.

formulaic expressions 7

Formulaic expressions are set, routinised phrases which are learned and used as whole units and which help with ease of communication. For example, 'at the end of the day', 'see what I mean', 'Further to your letter' are formulaic expressions.

fronting 61

Fronting occurs when words are placed for emphasis at the beginning of a clause or sentence. For example, in the sentence 'Beer I like but I can't drink wine at all', the word 'beer' is fronted.

genre 13

Genre is a term used to describe the intended goal or outcome of a particular speech event. For example, a lecture, a report, a narrative or an argument can be individual genres. In each case the genre will be marked by a particular set of language forms and structures. A narrative is normally marked by a simple past tense, a report by the passive voice, and so on.

graphic 7

A term used to refer to the physical process of making marks on a page or a screen. The related term graphology is conventionally used to refer to a study of styles of handwriting, of written print, or of computer imaging. The term graphological can be used as well as graphic.

graphology 7

The visual aspects of texts including lay-out and images.

idiolect 43

The term idiolect refers to an individually distinctive style of speaking.

impersonal noun 104

Nouns which refer to inanimate and non-personal entities are impersonal nouns, for example, 'instrument', or 'cargo'.

intertextuality 96

The way in which one text echoes or explicitly refers to another text.

lexis 55

Lexis is another term for vocabulary. However, a lexical item such as 'post-box' or 'smell a rat' (to be suspicious) can consist of more than one word.

metalanguage 7

Metalanguage is the language

used to talk and write about language and usually consists of a range of technical terms.

morpheme 34

A morpheme is a basic unit of grammar which marks out distinctions in meaning. For example, the verb 'walks' contains two morphemes, 'walk' and 's', the latter morpheme marking the person and tense of the verb.

passive (voice) 104

The passive voice shows that the subject in a sentence is the agent of the action or is affected by the action, e.g. 'Man is bitten by dog.'

phatic talk 28

Phatic talk is talk for social and interpersonal purposes rather than for transmitting information.

phonemes 30

The distinctive units of sound in a language.

prosody 88

Prosody or prosodic devices include features such as stress, rhythm and intonation which are used by speakers to mark out key meanings in a message.

reference 9

The act of referring to something. Anaphoric reference points backwards, e.g. the pronoun 'she' in the sentence 'I saw the girl; she was wearing . . .'. Cataphoric reference points forward, e.g the pronoun 'here' in the sentence, 'Here is the nine o'clock news.'

sub-skill 7

Sub-skills collectively make up skills, for example, the sub-skills of writing include punctuation and spelling.

synonym 5

Words with similar meanings are synonyms, for example, 'cheap'/'inexpensive' or 'fire'/'blaze'.

tag question 65

Tag questions are strings of words which are normally added to a declarative sentence to turn the statement into a question, for example 'It's very expensive to live there, *is it*?'

transactional 13

Transactional language is language to get things done or to transmit content and information rather than language for interpersonal or social purposes.

vague language 63

Vague language is more common in spoken than in written language. It is used to make statements sound imprecise and unassertive. Phrases such as 'sort of', 'like', 'and so on' or 'or whatever' are vague expressions.

references

Brazil, D. (1995) *A Grammar of Speech*, Oxford: Oxford University Press.

Carter, R., Goddard, A., Reah, D., Sanger, K. and Bowring, M. (2001) *Working with Texts: A Core Book in Language Analysis*, 2nd edn, London: Routledge.

Carter, R. and McCarthy, M. (1997) *Exploring Spoken English*, Cambridge: Cambridge University Press.

Chambers English Dictionary (1989), 7th edn, Edinburgh: W & R Chambers Ltd & Cambridge University Press.

Crystal, D. (1994) *The Cambridge Encyclopedia of Language*, Cambridge: Cambridge University Press.

Crystal, D. (date unknown) *English Now*, BBC Radio 4.

Graddol, D., Cheshire, J. and Swann, J. (1994) 2nd edn, *Describing Language*, Buckingham: Open University Press.

Hudson, R. (1984) *Higher Level Differences between Speech and Writing*, London: Committee for Linguistics in Education.

Kennedy, A.J. (1999) *The Rough Guide to the Internet*, London: Penguin Books.

New Shorter Oxford English Dictionary (1997), online version 1.0.03.

Pridham, F. (2001) *The Language of Conversation*, London: Routledge.

Sanger, K. (2000) *The Language of Drama*, London: Routledge.

Shakespeare, W. (1969) *Shakespeare Complete Works*, Oxford: Oxford University Press.

Tolkien, J.R.R. (1966) *The Hobbit*, London: Unwin Books.